INFORMATION AND COMMUN TECHNOLOGY

Intermediate GNVQ

INFORMATION AND COMMUNICATION TECHNOLOGY

Intermediate GNVQ

Tina Cross
and
Collette Jones

An imprint of **Pearson Education**

Harlow, England · London · New York · Reading, Massachusetts · San Francisco · Toronto · Don Mills, Ontario · Sydney
Tokyo · Singapore · Hong Kong · Seoul · Taipei · Cape Town · Madrid · Mexico City · Amsterdam · Munich · Paris · Milan

Pearson Education Limited
Edinburgh Gate
Harlow
Essex CM20 2JE, England
and Associated Companies throughout the world

ISBN 0 582 35707-1

British Library Cataloguing-in-Publication Data

A catalogue record for this book is available from the British Library.

Set by 30 in 10/12 Palatino
Printed in Malaysia, LSP

Contents

Preface

This book is written for students following the Edexcel, City and Guilds or Oxford, Cambridge and RSA (OCR) GNVQ Information and Communications Technology at Intermediate level. The structure of the book is based upon that of the syllabus and covers the three compulsory units as specified by the Qualifications and Curriculum Authority.

In response to requests we have included a separate section on programming. This text does not have the space to be the definitive guide to programming and we can only give a flavour of the possibilities. The students will need access to Visual Basic for Applications in Microsoft ® Excel to create the application used in this section.

This is a broad subject touching on many aspects of information and communications technology. To gain the award students will have to cover the three compulsory units and three further optional units.

In each unit, we have covered the underpinning knowledge required by the students to enable them to achieve the assessment evidence. Students must read and refer to the syllabus to ensure they keep in mind the material they must cover.

Within the book there are various activities that will be useful in assisting the student to apply the material.

This book is not intended to be used without the guidance and assistance of a teacher or tutor. We have not included detailed assessment activities within the book as these may depend upon the resources and facilities available to the student

Finally, we would like to thank our colleagues for their support during the time we were writing this book, the students who inspired us to write it and our families and friends for their tolerance.

Thanks also to Bob Jones for the photographs, Darren Maylor for the drawings, and to Microsoft for permission to include the screen dumps and examples used.

To those who provided the necessary encouragement to scale the wall, many thanks indeed.

Acknowledgement

Screen shots reprinted with permission from Microsoft Corporation.

Introduction

This book will provide you with the information you need in studying toward the GNVQ Information and Communications Technology at Intermediate level.

This qualification is a GCSE level course equivalent to four GCSEs at grade C or above. It is designed to enable you to develop a variety of skills in the field of Information and Communications Technology (ICT).

The skills you will learn include:

- How to present information
- How to handle information
- Understanding the forms of software and hardware

You will study six units of which three are compulsory and three are chosen from a list of options.

To be an effective student you will need a lively and enquiring mind with a particular interest in the wide area of ICT. You should enjoy exploring new ideas and communicating effectively with others. You will possibly not yet have decided in what area of Information and Communications Technology you wish to specialise.

Most of the units will be assessed by assignments set by your school or college. The compulsory unit, Presenting Information, will be assessed by work set externally as will one of the optional units.

The assessment work may be in the form of material you prepare in class before an examination style question paper. The questions will be about the material you worked on in class. You will take the prepared work into the exam room to enable you to use this in your answers. This work will then be handed in with your answers for assessment.

In this book we will concentrate on the compulsory units. All the information you will need is here. Each section covers all areas of the syllabus for that unit. There is guidance on the material you need for your assessment. You will find lots of activities throughout the book for you to do, including finding further information and discussing points raised with your classmates. We include many diagrams and illustrations to help you understand. There is also a section about programming. This will help you to write your own programs.

Unit 1 – Presenting information

This unit introduces you to the various styles of writing and presentation, types of information used, presentation and layout techniques, and the standard ways of working with documents.

This unit may be taught together with Unit 2, Handling information.

Unit 2 – Handling information

In this unit you learn what information handling means and how it is used. This covers the types of information handling, from newspapers to the Internet, the handling techniques used, the design of information handling systems, databases and spreadsheets, and standard ways of working with information handling.

Unit 3 – Hardware and software

This unit enables you to learn the various forms and functions of hardware and software. It teaches the basics of computer programming. You will create your own applications using macros. The section gives an understanding of HTML programs, as used in the creation of web pages on the Internet. The unit also provides an overview of the standard ways of working in this area.

Programming

This section will help you learn to write your own programs. It is unique to this book and will be of great interest to many of you.

We will use Visual Basic for Applications, a readily available language that many of you will have attached to the word processor or spreadsheet package that you use. We will show you how to further customise these and to improve your work.

Key Skills

You will probably be encouraged to work toward the Key Skills certification at levels 1, 2 or 3. During your work for Intermediate GNVQ in ICT you will develop your Key Skills in the following areas:

- Communication
- Application of number
- Information technology (IT)
- Problem solving
- Working with others
- Improving own learning and performance

The work you place in your portfolio will offer you the opportunity to develop and collect evidence for these Key Skills, although it will not cover every aspect. You may also find other opportunities occurring during lessons, individual study and other activities you undertake outside school or college. By studying and achieving the three compulsory units in GNVQ Intermediate ICT you will also achieve the Key Skill unit for IT at level 2.

In preparing and completing the coursework required you will also provide evidence that you can claim the Key Skills in Communication and Application of Number, provided you also pass the external test set by the awarding body. You can combine this together with other work you do for the optional units to claim the Key Skills units.

For example you may take part in a discussion or role-play, this could provide evidence for part of your **Communication** Key Skill. You will write reports as part of your course that may also provide evidence. You will be asked to collect and analyse information, this may then be used toward the **Application of Number** Key Skill. As you will use IT to present some of your coursework, you are also providing evidence for the **Information Technology** Key Skill.

Grades

Each unit of work you perform during your studies will be awarded a grade. These grades are Below pass, Pass, Merit or Distinction. At the end of the course your whole portfolio of work will be given a grade, these are also Below pass, Pass, Merit or Distinction.

Each unit will be awarded a grade to which points are allocated.

Below pass	Pass	Merit	Distinction
0 – 6	7 – 9	10 – 12	13 – 16

These will then be added together to give your portfolio grade. The grades will be awarded as follows.

Below pass	Pass	Merit	Distinction
0 – 41	42 – 59	60 – 77	78 – 96

You should refer to the syllabus to see exactly what is required for you to be awarded each of these grades. There is a copy of the unit grade descriptors at the end of each section.

Progression

At the end of your course you will have access to a range of career and further education opportunities. You will have learned a variety of skills throughout the course, including collecting, analysing and interpreting data, communicating your findings in different ways, and identifying and developing the links between different parts of the subject. All these skills are recognised and highly valued by employers and colleges alike.

You have a great opportunity to study a range of skills within the Information and Communications Technology area, we hope you will enjoy it. This is a growing area in all our lives. Less than ten years ago mobile phones were quite rare and rather bulky but now they are small and light and many people have them. This is an indication of the rapid changes we are all seeing in our lives, brought about by Information and Communications Technology.

Unit 1

PRESENTING INFORMATION

Introduction

This unit is designed to help you to use information technology to produce documents of your own. After working through this unit you will be able to:

- Write original documents to suit your readers
- Improve the accuracy and quality of documents that you create
- Choose and apply standard layouts
- Understand some standard ways of working
- Understand some of the ways organisations present information
- Understand why organisations use a wide range of standard documents
- Develop good practice in your use of IT

This unit looks at the ways in which documents are written to suit the reader. We will see how the accuracy and general quality may be ensured. We shall look at the layouts that may be used to standardise documents and the methods of working that assist in this. Other topics will include the ways in which organisations present information and the reasons why they use different documents. During all this we shall discuss various aspects of good practice in the use of IT.

You will find it helpful to collect samples of documents designed for a variety of different purposes and from different sources. This will help you to develop your understanding of the various documents.

We shall look at the area under the following topics:

- Standard documents and their purposes
- Suitability of the prepared documents
- Accuracy of information
- Presentation techniques
- Standard ways of working
- Organisations and their use of information
- Security procedures

Standard documents and their purpose

Communication is an essential element in all our lives, and in business life in particular. We shall look at a variety of items used for the presentation of information:

- Formal letters
- Newspaper advertisements
- Flyers
- Informal notes
- Formal invitations
- Questionnaires
- Tables of results
- Reports
- Drafts

Each of these are very different ways in which to communicate information. Most people will have the opportunity to read each, in a variety of different areas of their lives.

In writing for different audiences and media we must consider the needs of the reader and the message we wish to convey. We will look at the writing styles and presentation methods employed in:

- Memos
- Flyers
- Drafts
- Business cards
- Business letters
- Newsletters
- Faxes
- E-mails (electronic mail)
- Reports

Organisations need to communicate with the world outside their business – with their customers and their suppliers. Organisations also need to communicate with various legal bodies, such as the tax authorities.

Activity

What information will be passed from an organisation to their customers and suppliers? What information will be received from suppliers and customers?

Organisations need to communicate internally – information must pass between the members of the organisation. Much of this communication may be on paper, using a range of documents.

You may have heard of the memo, short for memorandum, a word from Latin meaning remembrance. Memos are used as a means of communicating short amounts of information around an organisation. A memo is informal, in that it does not start with 'Dear' as a letter might, and is usually on some form of headed paper. It is also unsigned, although the name and title of the sender will be included in the heading.

Businesses communicate with their customers by means of documents such as:

- Business letters
- Business cards
- Faxes
- Invoices
- Customer newsletters

Activity

List what information might be included in each of these.

Such communications tend to be of a formal nature. These documents are used to convey specific information to the recipients. For example, a newsletter may be used to inform customers about new products or services. The layout may be similar to that shown in Figure 1.1.

Fig. 1.1 A typical layout for a newsletter

 ## Activity

What would the other documents be used for? Find one example of each.

These documents also have another function. They are an important means of establishing and maintaining the identity of an organisation and will usually be produced with a distinctive house style (or corporate image). The stationery used for these documents will carry the organisation's logo, reinforcing this in the mind of the recipient. Business letters are usually printed on high quality paper to create an image of quality in a customer's mind.

Activity

Have a look at some business letters you or your family have received. What styles are used in these letters? These will be useful in your studies, keep them.

Here are a variety of other documents used by organisations:

- Memoranda
- Meeting agenda
- Meeting minutes
- Reports
- E-mails
- Internal newsletters

Activity

Collect some examples to study. What is each used for? What styles are used?

These documents are used largely for internal communications and range from the informal memorandum, or memo, through to the formal report. These too will conform to the organisation's house style, helping to create and reinforce a sense of corporate identity among the members of the organisation.

Formal letters

After you have finished your studies you will, perhaps, be looking for work. In doing this you will send formal letters to those organisations to whom you are applying for a position. In such a letter you will not 'chat' to the reader as you might to a friend. Your letter will need to:

- Attract attention
- Set out facts clearly
- Explain to the potential employer why you should be considered for the position

In attracting attention you will bear in mind:

- Your probable reader
- That you want to prove yourself an asset to the organisation and not a liability

In considering your reader you must acknowledge how much they will have to read. You must ensure your letter is not so long or boring as to lose the attention of the reader. The information you present must be summarised in such a way as not to lose impact but to explain in sufficient detail to be useful.

There are other types of formal letter. They include letters between organisations, perhaps requesting information or services. Organisations may also receive formal letters complaining about the quality of services or goods.

Activity

Have you, or any member of your family, needed to write such a letter? Try to write a letter of complaint. Imagine you have bought a brand new computer from a mail order company. When you unpacked it there was no power cable and there were two printer power cables. You must state what is wrong and what you want the organisation to do to correct this.

For some people the most interesting parts of newspapers are the letters from readers. These are usually addressed to the editor although the writers intend them to be for publication and so to be read by a variety of people. The tone of these letters will vary depending on the subject matter, the type of publication and the writers' feelings.

Activity

Read the letters pages in a variety of publications. Could you identify the publication from the letter alone? Choose a subject of interest to you and write a letter to the editor of the appropriate publication.

Companies generally produce business letters on stationery that has been preprinted with the organisation's logo, address, telephone number in the style chosen by the organisation. Figure 1.2 shows a typical layout.

The letter starts with the date. Under this is the name and address of the recipient. Note that there is no punctuation in the address – this is the accepted style. In this example, the recipient's name is known, so it is appropriate for the salutation to be 'Dear Mr Jones'. If the letter is not being addressed to a named individual, 'Dear Sir' should be used. All the text is 'blocked' at the left margin and a blank line is left between each paragraph. The letter ends with the complimentary close 'Yours sincerely', space for a signature and the name and position of the writer. If the 'Dear Sir' had been used, the complimentary close 'Yours faithfully' would have been used.

Figure 1.3 shows another possible layout. In this example, the date is positioned to the right of the recipient's address and the letter includes a reference, which usually consists of the writer's and typist's initials. The use of the more formal salutation and close is shown.

ABC Printers Ltd
64 High Street
Anytown
A46 8TY

Telephone: 0156 987213

2 October 2000

Mr DS Jones
Angel Computing Ltd
92 Birdcage Road
Anytown
A23 9ZW

Dear Mr Jones

Thank you for your enquiry about the design and printing of business cards and other stationery for your company.

Enclosed are some samples of material which we produce and our current price list. I will contact you in the next few days to arrange a meeting to discuss your requirements in more detail.

Yours sincerely

JF Brown
Sales Manager

Fig. 1.2 A business letter to a named recipient

Newspaper advertisements

You or your family may have had second-hand goods for sale. Often these are advertised in newspapers. The cost of the advertisement depends on the amount of space taken up, so items are usually advertised in very few words while still trying to sound attractive.

ABC Printers Ltd
64 High Street
Anytown
A46 8TY

Telephone: 0156 987213

Supplies Manager   2 October 2000
Angel Computing Ltd   Ref: JFB/CJ
92 Birdcage Road
Anytown
A23 9ZW

Dear Sir

Thank you for your enquiry about the design and printing of business cards and
other stationery for your company.

Enclosed are some samples of material which we produce and our current price list.
I will contact you in the next few days to arrange a meeting to discuss your
requirements in more detail.

Yours faithfully

JF Brown
Sales Manager

Fig. 1.3 A business letter to a recipient whose name is not known

Activity

**Read some classified advertisements and see which are effective and which are
not. Choose an item and write an advert for your local paper to sell this. Will it
attract the attention you need?**

Perhaps you or a member of your family have bought, or are considering buying, a car. You may be in the market for a brand new car. The advertisements for new cars are often on a full page. There will usually be a large photograph of the new car and a list of the features that the advertisers feel will appeal to you as a potential buyer. These features will be different today to those advertised 20 years ago. We are now concerned as a society with ecological and financial issues. Therefore, the amount of fossil fuel used is of interest, as is the type of fuel used. In the past a new car would be launched showing a scantily clad pretty girl draped over it. In these days of equality this is no longer acceptable. Women now buy their own vehicles and influence the purchases of other members of their circle, so advertisers aim their advertising at women as well as men.

Activity

What is it that attracts your eye? Collect advertisements of new cars and compare them. What items are commonly listed as sales features? What benefits to the purchaser are they advertising?

Flyers

Some organisations use flyers to advertise their products or services. You have seen many of these, inserted as loose leaflets into magazines, newspapers, delivered through the door or stuck under windscreen wipers in car parks.

Activity

Collect some flyers. Which are effective and which are not? Why?

Informal notes

Many times in our lives we need to use informal notes. You may take a telephone message for another member of your family. If you then have to go out, what do you do with that message? You may scribble a note and leave it beside the telephone, or on the table. Anywhere it will be noticed.

Activity

Where do your family leave such messages? Collect some examples for your studies.

A child may become unwell and require to be kept home from school. To explain this absence the parent or guardian will send a note to the school. Such a note is formal, as it is entered in the school records, but will be addressed personally to either the head teacher or the class teacher, e.g. Dear Mrs Jones. The note will be brief and to the point. To close, the parent may do no more than sign the note. There is no real need to treat the document as a formal letter and very few will.

Activity

Compare the informal note shown in Figure 1.4 to a formal letter, such as that shown in Figure 1.3. Identify the differences.

Formal invitations

Invitations occur in a variety of different situations and circumstances. A friend may telephone and invite you round for dinner. This is an informal invitation. You will usually accept this by simply saying 'yes' during the conversation. There is no need to write a letter of acceptance, although it is polite to write a note of thanks afterwards.

Activity

When was the last time you received an informal invitation? List a few examples.

Invitations to weddings are often issued formally. These invitations may be printed on card, with the recipients' name written in by the hosts. The recipient is expected to send a letter either accepting or refusing the invitation.

Activity

Have you or your family received such an invitation? How was the invitation worded?

It might have been worded like the invitation shown in Figure 1.5.

Gone to meet Jill.

Back around 4.30, will bring the tea.

Tina

Fig. 1.4 An informal note

Mr and Mrs Richard Jones request the pleasure of the
company of

Mr & Mrs Keith Georgiadas and Janet

on the occasion of the marriage of their daughter Julie to
Mr John Smith at 11 o'clock in St James Church on Saturday
16th September 2000

Fig. 1.5 A wedding invitation

Activity

Have a look in stationers' sample books to see the sorts of designs and wording used.

Questionnaires

You may have found yourself out shopping on a Saturday, drifting through the crowd, oops too late, the opinion poll person has caught you. Or perhaps the pollsters have sent their questions through the post to you.

Activity

What is the layout of the questionnaire like? What sort of answers are you encouraged to give, yes/no, or sentences? What incentives are they offering for you to complete and return the poll?

There may be the offer of an entry in a draw, or some other prize or reward for returning the completed questionnaire.

Questionnaires are usually used to collect large quantities of simple data, e.g. how many of the sample (the group of people questioned) support a particular football club, political party or use a particular product. The questions are usually phrased to encourage very simple answers. They may encourage yes or no responses. They may be set as a series of statements and the reader has to indicate how much they agree or disagree with the statements.

Activity

Consider how you might use a questionnaire, perhaps to do a survey on how other students arrive at school or college. What do you want to know? How would you go about finding out what you want to know?

In the above activity you should start by listing what you need to know. For example:

- How far from college or school do individuals live?
- How many live less than 1 mile?
- How many live less than 3 miles?
- How many live less than 5 miles?
- How many live less than 10 miles?
- How many live more than 10 miles?
- How many walk in?
- How many ride bicycles?
- How many drive cars?
- How many are driven in by family or friends?
- How many use public transport?
- How many use buses?
- How many use trains?

To collect the information we need we must also consider how we are going to use it. Consider the travel survey, you may want to discover the proportion of students who travel in an 'ecologically friendly' manner.

You need to be able to categorise the answers. To make this easier you must direct the respondent to particular answers. If you ask, 'What sort of transport do you use?' the respondent may reply with a variety of answers. Therefore, you will need to ask a 'closed' question such as, 'Do you walk to college/school?' This closed question allows only 'yes' or 'no' as an answer. You may feel that the number of questions you need to ask is greater using this method but the results are more easily analysed.

Another consideration is how to deliver the questionnaires. Are you going to hand them out at random as people arrive or leave the venue? If you do this how many will complete the form and return it? Why should they? Perhaps it would be better to stop individuals and question them at random while they are on campus?

Let us go back to the opinion poll person. Consider all the questionnaires they gather in a day or week or perhaps for an entire study.

Activity

How might the results be presented?

Tables of results

Many people follow sports such as football, rugby or darts that are organised into leagues. This ensures individuals and teams are matched against similar standard players to make more interesting competition. They will compete to lead the league. The aim is to be at the top of the league and not be relegated to the lower leagues.

Do you follow such a sport? How are the results posted? Most frequently they will be posted in a table, each member of the league listed according to their position in the league.

Compare league results. How do you determine your favourite teams' position? In football, teams get points for every league game they win or draw. The number of points for a win is determined by whether they are playing 'at home' or 'away'.

Activity

What are the column headings in a football league table?

Perhaps you follow Formula 1 motor racing.

Activity

How does a driver win the Drivers Championship? What other championships are there in Formula 1? How is the winner in this decided upon?

Reports

Many organisations are managed by one controlling body. In some commercial organisations it is the Board of Directors, in a school it is the Board of Governors. The country is an organisation run by Government. The various responsibilities are delegated to different committees, who will then report to the controlling body. These reports are an important part of the decision-making process.

For example, the local authority has many responsibilities including education, rubbish collection and highway maintenance. Among the responsibilities are those for the control and management of building in the area. Should anyone wish to build a house, a planning application must be made. This will then be inspected and investigated by employees of the planning authority who will then report to the planning committee. The committee will consider the application using the reports from the specialists who will have included a recommendation to accept or reject. The committee may follow the recommendation or not as they see fit, provided they adhere to the law. They may decide to grant an application but attach conditions, perhaps they grant a change of use to farmland to a commercial nursery but insist that the entrance is widened to make access to the highway easier.

Activity

Read your local papers and see what planning applications are presented. Choose one and follow it through to the decision. The committee minutes are open to the public and give the reasons why a project is accepted or rejected.

Drafts

Many items for publication, including this book, are first written in rough form, to enable the writer and editor to concentrate on the text. When in draft form a document will be read to ensure it is correct and amended where necessary. This is called proof-reading.

In the draft form a document may be presented on paper. If this is the case the line spacing will be set to double and the margins all around should be at least 4 cms to allow for the addition of corrections. Among the corrections will be spelling and grammar, together with improvements in the text.

When you prepare your work for presentation you should also print a draft copy to check the text for spelling mistakes and grammar. Although all modern word processing packages include spell and grammar checkers, it is not sufficient to simply run these. If you merely accept the first suggestion offered you may well find that the wrong word is chosen. For, instance, if you type, 'wich' the spell check will suggest a list of words starting, 'which, witch'. However, only you can decide which is correct, as you can understand the context, or meaning, the word processor cannot.

This is particularly true when using the grammar checker. For instance, if you select the wrong 'correction' from the checker it might change entirely the meaning you were trying to convey to the reader.

Suitability of prepared documents

Document design is often the job of a graphic designer, who will design a range of stationery for the various documents an organisation will use or the layout of a newsletter. When the design has been agreed, members of the organisation are given instructions telling them how to produce each type of document.

These instructions may be in paper form – a diagram showing the required layout. Alternatively, the document design may be provided as a template with the necessary information incorporated. Macros may also be written to help the users to produce the documents.

A template is a file that is used as the basis for others. It will contain such details as the page set-up information, the various styles used for the text and information about other items, for instance the headers and footers. All this is explained in more detail in Unit 3 – Hardware and Software.

Macros may also be written to help the users to produce the documents. Macros are programs written for use within the application the user is using, e.g. a word processor. See Unit 3 for a detailed description of what a macro is.

An example macro code is shown in Figure 1.6. This is designed to call the appropriate template and ask the user for the required data before placing the cursor ready for further input.

Activity

Note how the code is broken into sections and each is labelled as to purpose. Why do you think this is done?

To be effective, a document must be well designed. The layout must be attractive and the text easy to read. If the first impression of a document is poor, the

```
Sub Letter()
' Macro to set up letter created 08/05/99 by Tina Cross
'
' Running requirements:- template called Letter.dot at specified location.
'
' Open letter template and move cursor to end
'
    Documents.Add Template:= _"C:\Program Files\Microsoft
    Office\Templates\Letters & Faxes\Letter.dot" _, NewTemplate:=False
    Selection.EndKey Unit:=wdLine
    Selection.TypeParagraph
    Selection.TypeParagraph
'
' Request and accept user input of addressee name
'
    Selection.TypeText Text:=InputBox("Insert Addressee name, e.g. Mr J
    Bloggs", "Letter")
    Selection.TypeParagraph
'
' Request and accept user address details line by line
'
    Selection.TypeText Text:=InputBox("Insert house name/road, e.g. 34 Pretty
    Lane", "Letter")
    Selection.TypeParagraph
    Selection.TypeText Text:=InputBox("Insert district, e.g. Westside",
    "Letter")
    Selection.TypeParagraph
    Selection.TypeText Text:=InputBox("Insert town, e.g. Westown", "Letter")
    Selection.TypeParagraph
    Selection.TypeText Text:=InputBox("Insert county, e.g. Westshire",
    "Letter")
    Selection.TypeParagraph
    Selection.TypeText Text:=InputBox("Insert postcode, e.g. WE43 23DR",
    "Letter")
    Selection.TypeParagraph
'
' Move cursor down 2 lines and input salutation
'
    Selection.TypeParagraph
    Selection.TypeParagraph
    Selection.TypeText Text:="Dear"
'
' Request and accept user input of addressee
'
    Selection.TypeText Text:=InputBox("Insert addressee name, e.g. Joe",
    "Letter")
    Selection.TypeParagraph
    Selection.TypeParagraph

End Sub
```

Fig. 1.6 Sample macro code

recipient is likely to judge the sender in the same way. For example if you receive a letter that is full of typing errors or spelling mistakes you are likely to assume that the sender is slipshod in the way that they work. The letter then advertises the sender's attitude to their work. This is why you should be careful about the presentation of your coursework.

When a document is designed, the first thing that must be considered is its purpose. For example, a customer newsletter and an invoice serve different functions and will need very different formats. Once the purpose of a document has been decided, many other design features, such as paper size and text layout, will follow from this.

Activity

Look at the documents you collected earlier. Are they suited to their purpose? See if you can identify what makes a document suit its purpose and what does not.

When creating documents for yourself you must consider the purpose of the document. What do you need to say? To whom are you addressing your communication? Is it a formal letter, an informal e-mail to a colleague, a newspaper advertisement, or a report on the decisions made in a committee? Each has different information that you want to impart to the reader.

In a job application you will want to inform the reader of:

● Your name and address
● The post for which you are applying
● Your educational qualifications
● The skills you have that suit you for the post

Activity

Write a letter of application for a job in a hospital IT department as a junior on the help desk. Your letter should be addressed to the Personnel Officer of Health and Hope Hospital. Create a draft first to hone the text and to check your spelling and grammar. Then consider the layout of the letter – using the word processor you should use a fully blocked letter.

Next let's look at writing an advertisement.

Activity

Choose an object and write an advertisement to be placed in your local paper. Remember that you pay for space but need to attract attention.

In an advertisement you will need to:

● Briefly describe the object for sale
● Describe its advantages over other similar items
● Indicate the price required
● Give contact details for interested people to use

Activity

Which advertisements in your local paper appeal to you? Why? Compare your advert to those you selected. How do you think you could improve it?

We can see that writing a letter of application for a job is very different to writing a newspaper advertisement. The language you use to communicate with the potential employer will be very different to that of the newspaper advertisement. Verbosity or wordiness may be possible in the letter of application. However, with newspaper advertisements you are paying for space; more words, more space, more cost.

Accuracy of information

All documents are created to communicate a message. The important thing is to capture the reader's attention. Having interested your reader, you can then communicate your message.

Activity

Write another advert to sell a second-hand bicycle. Remember that you will pay by the word, but you must make it sound worth a look to anyone who is interested.

Documents need to be checked to make sure that the data given in them is correct. For example, if you are preparing a business letter, it is very important that it's addressed correctly, i.e. to the correct person, correct address and postcode. If not, the letter may not reach its intended recipient. It is also important that any mis-spellings and typing errors are corrected. Documents with spelling mistakes and typing errors may be irritating to the reader and can create a bad impression.

You should 'proof' all your documents, this means you should check them for spelling, grammar and layout. Most people find it easier to check a printed document rather than one displayed on a computer screen. Therefore, the document should be printed out as a draft (using the draft output from the printer on lesser quality paper) and carefully read through, looking for any mistakes. It is useful to mark corrections on this printed version so that all the alterations can be made at the same time. The next printout can be improved against the marked draft. This proof-reading should be done very carefully. It is very easy to miss small errors and to read what you expect to see rather than what is actually printed on the page.

Try doing this with all your coursework. You will be pleased with the result, and so will your assessor!

Most word processing software includes tools to help you to find mistakes. These tools include:

- Spell checker
- Grammar checker
- Thesaurus

Many word processors can be set to automatically invoke these tools so that the user does not need to remember to call upon them while working.

Activity

Investigate the package you use. Can any of these tools be set to work automatically? Switch it on, enter some text, with mistakes, and watch what happens. Now try with the automatic facility switched off but using the same text. What is the difference?

Spell checking

Spell checking facilities can help you to reduce the number of spelling mistakes and typing errors. The words in the document are checked against a dictionary and any words not found in the dictionary are highlighted for possible correction. Most spell checkers also suggest alternative spellings for words that are not found in the dictionary. It may also be possible to add words to the dictionary or to create your own personal dictionary. You might want to do this if you often use technical terms that are not included in the standard dictionary. A word of warning – always check the spelling of any word you plan to add to your dictionary – don't add misspelt words!

When using any spell checker you must be aware that it may not find all errors. For example, if you use the word 'there' instead of 'their' the spell checker will not notice as the word is correctly spelt.

If your software has spell checking facilities you should use them. There is no excuse when using modern software for producing documents that are full of typing and spelling mistakes. These can be so easily found and corrected.

Grammar checking

Most grammar checker tools can be set to different styles, e.g. for business or casual writing. The checker scans the text in your document and identifies sentences that contain possible grammatical or stylistic errors and suggests ways in which they could be improved. You may accept this advice or reject it. It may be that the suggestion changes the meaning of the sentence or is just not an appropriate style for the piece you are writing. It is also possible that the checker brings up as errors, terms that are quite correct.

Activity

Using a variety of texts, run a grammar checker and see what difference the various style settings make. Can you guess the results?

Thesaurus

You may need a synonym (a word of similar meaning) or an autonym (a word of opposite meaning). The thesaurus tool will help you find alternative words, quickly.

When writing anything it is wise to avoid using the same word too often. For example, would you want to read on if a story started, 'The sun was bright and shone on the bright colours of the flowers'.

The thesaurus enables you to expand your vocabulary with ease, and you can be confident that the words offered are appropriate. It is wise to use a dictionary if you are in any doubt as to the exact meaning of a word that you may wish to use. The English language has the largest vocabulary of all modern languages and it is prudent to use it with care. As an example we are all aware of the difference in meaning between the words 'love' and 'like'. However, many other languages only make the distinction by the context in which the word is used.

Activity

Use the thesaurus on words with which you are familiar. Are the results what you expected? Look up any unfamiliar words in a dictionary.

Other tools

Most word processors also include tools to count words and judge the readability of the document.

Let us suppose you have to write an essay or an article for a newspaper. It may be that a particular length is required, e.g. 2,000 words. By using the word count tool you can ensure you do not fall too short or write too much.

Having written your article the readability statistics will give an indication of how easy the article is to read. The shorter the sentences and the simpler the words you use the greater the level of readability achieved.

Activity

Try out these tools for yourself and see the results on your work.

Presentation techniques

Activity

Look at the documents you have collected. Sort them into categories according to how good they are at performing their task.
Compare a good example with a poor one and try to identify what makes the difference.

To create an effective document there are many design items which must be considered. Some may be dictated by the document itself. For example, a formal letter will usually require white or cream paper. Coloured paper is not considered 'good form', but would be ideal for a flyer. Having decided the medium then the wording must be settled and, if appropriate, pictures chosen.

Most commercial documents will be produced using word processing software. There are many different word processing packages available to choose from. Many of the packages will run on a standalone computer such as a PC.

Word processing packages provide a range of functions that allow the user to produce documents combining text, data and graphic information. The exact commands which will need to be used will vary from package to package. You need to consult the user manuals and the on-line help for your particular software package for details of the commands you will need to use.

Most documents will consist largely of text which is entered using the computer keyboard. Documents may also contain tables of data and graphic information such as charts and pictures. These document elements will need to be arranged appropriately on the page.

Page attributes

There are two page attributes to be considered:

- Paper size
- Orientation

Paper size

There are standard paper sizes in general use. Common paper sizes are:

- A3 297×420 mm
- A4 210×297 mm
- A5 148×210 mm

As can be seen from Figure 1.7 and the measurements above, two pages of A5 side by side are equivalent to one page of A4. Similarly two pages of A4 are equivalent to one of A3.

Activity

How big are the sizes A2, A1 and A0? How did you work this out?

Of these sizes, A4 is the one you will probably use most often. It is the standard size of paper used in most printers and photocopiers.

When you choose a paper size, you should think about the purpose of the document you are producing. Documents that are going to be filed in standard ring binders or files in a filing cabinet will probably be best produced on A4 paper. Posters that are to be displayed on notice boards will need to be larger and A3 might be a better size. A memo will probably only be a few lines and so A5 will be sufficient.

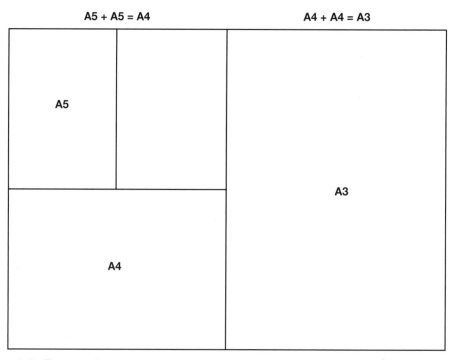

Fig. 1.7 Paper sizes

Orientation

Paper can be used in either of two orientations:

- Portrait
- Landscape

Figure 1.8 illustrates what these phrases mean.

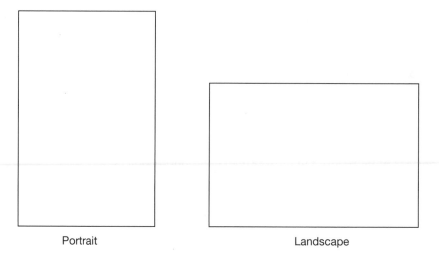

Portrait   Landscape

Fig. 1.8 Paper orientation

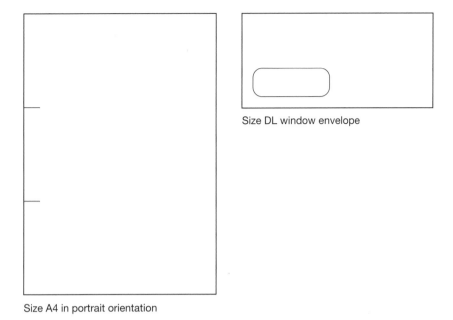

Size DL window envelope

Size A4 in portrait orientation

Fig. 1.9 A4 paper with DL envelope

Portrait is the most common orientation for documents, including letters. When you are making notes for your work it is natural for you to write on the paper using portrait orientation.

Consider how the standard A4 page will fold into three to fit neatly into the standard DL sized window envelope, allowing the address on the letter to show through the window (see Figure 1.9).

Landscape orientation is appropriate for pages containing wide tables, which would not fit a portrait page without cramping the text or using a very small font size. You may also see price lists and advertising flyers produced using three columns on paper in landscape orientation. This may then be folded into three.

Layout

Once you have selected a paper size and orientation, you will need to think about how the text is to be positioned on the page. In a simple document, you will need to consider:

- Margins
- Justification
- Indents
- Bullets
- Tabulations
- Line spacing
- Font style and size

In a more complex document, you may wish to use:

- Headers and footers
- Columns
- Page numbers

Margins

When creating any document you should consider how the page would look to your reader. The larger the area of white space you have the more likely the reader is to take in all the information on the page.

Margins are the spaces you leave at the top, bottom, left and right of the page. The margins set the boundaries for the text on the page (see Figure 1.10). They are part of the important element of any document known as the 'white space'.

Margins should be set so that the text can be laid out attractively on the page. If a document is single-sided (printed on only one side of the paper) and going to be filed in a ring binder or bound in some way, the left margin needs to be wide enough that the text is not hidden in the binding. If a document is printed on both

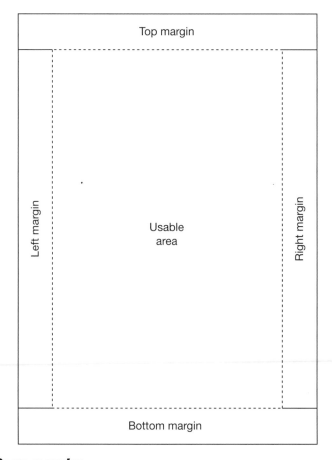

Fig. 1.10 Page margins

sides of the paper, then the page on the right will need the left margin wider while the page on the left will require the right margin to be the wider.

A long document, such as a report, may be printed on each side of the page and be bound into a folder. In this case, the appearance of the final document is improved if the outer margins of the pages are the same. To achieve this, different left and right margins will be needed for odd and even numbered pages. Some word processing packages make this adjustment automatically for you.

If you are using a header in a document, it will be printed in the top margin, so you will need to make sure that this margin is deep enough to accommodate the header. Similarly, footers are printed in the bottom margin.

If you are producing documents on stationery which has items such as a logo or an address preprinted on it, your margins will have to take into account the areas of the page that are already used in this way, to avoid printing over the top of this information.

Justification

This term refers to the alignment of text between the horizontal margins, the left and right margins of the page. Text is described as left justified, right justified or fully justified; it is also possible to centre text between the margins.

Left justification is the phrase used to indicate that the text is presented with a straight left-hand margin with the spacing between each word even and regular. The result may be a very regular and straight left-hand edge to the paragraph with the right-hand edge being irregular and 'ragged' (see Figure 1.11).

Right justification means the exact opposite, the word spacing is still the same as described above. The appearance of the paragraph is a very regular and straight right-hand edge with the left-hand edge being irregular and 'ragged' (see Figure 1.11).

Fully justified paragraphs look very squared off. To achieve the very straight margins to the left and right the software will adjust the spaces between each word to 'fill' each line of text out to the margins. This always looks very professional and is popular in all types of formal documents.

Finally, text may be centred horizontally between the left and right margins. Using this format you will find neither the left nor the right edges of the text will be straight. This has limited use, for example for headings or lists such as menus.

Indents

The modern convention is that text in a document, such as a letter or a report, is blocked to the left margin and a blank line is left between paragraphs. A paragraph may be highlighted by being indented. This is shown in Figure 1.12.

Books often use a different convention. The paragraphs are not separated by a blank line. Instead the first line of the paragraph is indented (see Figure 1.12).

Bullets

If you wish to list items in a document you may like to use bullets. Unnumbered lists may use a symbol (such as an arrow or other special character) on the left-hand side of the text with a space before the listed item. Alternatively you may need each item to be numbered, in which case you would use numbers instead.

This is left aligned text. This is left aligned text. This is left aligned text.This is left aligned text.

This is right aligned text. This is right aligned text. This is right aligned text.This is right aligned text.

This is justified text. This is justified text. This is justified text. This is justified text. This is justified text. This is justified text.

This is centred text. This is centred text. This is centred text.This is centred text.This is centred text.

Fig. 1.11 Examples of standard text justification

Activity

Investigate the software available to you to see how this is done and what bullet symbols are available to you.

Tabulations

Tab stops are used to set the position of text relative to the margins of the page. They are usually set up on the ruler at the top of the page. Pressing the Tab key moves the cursor to the next tab position.

Tabs can be used to align text in columns when typing simple tables. Left, right, centre and decimal point alignment are possible. These different alignments are shown in Figure 1.13.

> This is a standard paragraph, blocked to the left margin and justified. This is a standard paragraph, blocked to the left margin and justified. This is a standard paragraph, blocked to the left margin and justified.
>
>   This is an indented paragraph. This is an indented paragraph. This is an indented paragraph. This is an indented paragraph. This is an indented paragraph.
>
> This is a standard paragraph, blocked to the left margin and justified. This is a standard paragraph, blocked to the left margin and justified. This is a standard paragraph, blocked to the left margin and justified.

>   This paragraph has an indented first line and the paragraphs are not separated by blank lines. This paragraph has an indented first line and the paragraphs are not separated by blank lines.
>   This paragraph has an indented first line and the paragraphs are not separated by blank lines. This paragraph has an indented first line and the paragraphs are not separated by blank lines.
>   This paragraph has an indented first line and the paragraphs are not separated by blank lines. This paragraph has an indented first line and the paragraphs are not separated by blank lines.

Fig. 1.12 The types of indent used in reports (top) and in some books (bottom)

It is more common now for such tables of data to be positioned on the page using a table facility. This places a grid of 'boxes' onto the page. Each 'cell' may be justified according to the data to be placed in it. The grid may be invisible or have visible borders placed around it.

Line spacing

The spacing between the lines of text in a document can be varied. Most documents use single line spacing where there is type on every line. Other spacing is possible. Double line spacing, where there is a blank line after each line of text, is often used for draft documents where changes may need to be marked on the text.

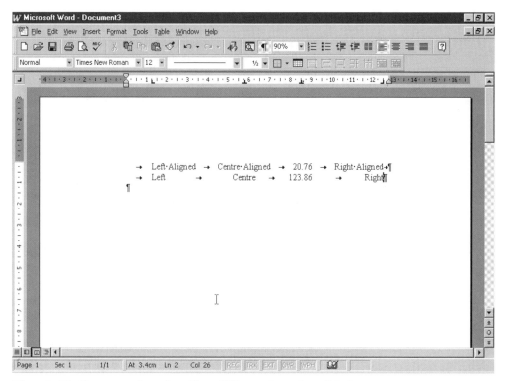

Fig. 1.13 Screen showing the different sorts of tabs

As well as setting the spaces between the lines, it is also possible to vary the spacing between paragraphs and before or after headings to make these stand out more.

Activity

What can be done with the software you have available to vary the spaces between lines of text? How do you set this?

Fonts

The design or shape of the characters used in a document is referred to as a font.

Each font will consist of a set of UPPER CASE characters (capital letters) and a set of lower case characters. In all the documents you produce each will have its place.

It is tempting in advertising pieces, or others which you wish to use to attract attention, to use all upper case characters to provide impact. However, research done for the advertising industry has provided evidence that we prefer to read the normal mixture of upper and lower case characters. It was also discovered that we often ignore pieces that don't conform to this expectation.

If we write H2O or e = mc2, you might work out what is meant, but, H_2O or e = mc^2 is much more clear. These characters above and below the 'normal' line of presentation clarify the issue.

The 2 in H_2O is a **subscript** character, that is one dropping below the base line of the rest of the characters. The numeral 2 in $e = mc^2$ is **superscript**, it is above the line. Superscript and subscript characters are often required in scientific and mathematical documents.

The two main types of font are called serif and sans serif. Serif fonts have small curves on the letters which lead the eye along the line of text, making it easier to read. Examples of serif fonts include Courier and Times New Roman. Sans serif fonts do not have these curves and have a very modern look. A typical sans serif font is Arial. These fonts are shown in Figure 1.14.

If you are writing a long piece you may choose to use both serif and sans serif fonts. The sans serif would be used for headings and subheadings with the bulk of the text using the serif font. This is a common convention in publishing.

Arial

Courier

Times New Roman

Arial 12 point

Arial 24 point

Arial 36 point

Arial 12 point normal

Arial 12 point bold

Arial 12 point italic

Arial 12 point bold italic

Fig. 1.14 Examples of font styles and sizes

Activity

Look in newspapers, magazines and books. Try to identify whether the fonts used are with or without the serif or 'tail' on the characters.

Figure 1.14 also shows another difference between types of font. Courier is an example of a fixed spaced font. This means that all the letters take the same amount of space along a line. A slim letter such as an 'i' will occupy the same space as a wide letter such as an 'm'. Text in a fixed spaced font looks 'typed'. The other fonts, Arial and Times New Roman, are examples of proportional spaced fonts. In these the space taken by each character is in proportion to its width, so an 'i' will occupy less space than an 'm' and the text will look 'printed'.

Each font can be produced in a range of sizes and styles. Some of these are shown in Figure 1.14.

Headers and footers

If you look at many textbooks and multipage documents, you will see that there is often information at the top and bottom of the pages. For example, the title of the chapter may be printed at the top of each page and the page numbers may be printed at the bottom outside corner of each page. This information is held in headers and footers. Figure 1.15 shows a page with a header and footer.

Chapter 1

This is the text of the document. This is the text of
the document with headers and footers to hold a
chapter number and a page number. This is the text
of the document. This is the text of the document
with headers and footers to hold a chapter number
and a page number.

Page 1

Fig. 1.15 A page showing a header and a footer which includes a page number

Most word processing packages allow you to set up and edit the text that will be used for a header or footer. This text is then added automatically to the pages when the document is printed. If your document will be printed on each side of the paper, you may need to set up different headers and footers for the odd and even pages. Headers and footers are positioned in the top and bottom margins of documents. It is important that the margins are set large enough to fit the headers and footers.

Activity

Investigate the word processing package you will use. How can you set up the headers and footers? What information will you put in them, for example in the production of your coursework?

Columns

Some documents are produced with the text and any graphics arranged in columns. A columnar format is very common for newsletters. Figure 1.1 (page 5) showed a possible layout for a newsletter produced in two columns.

Most packages allow you to set up a number of columns on a page, setting the width of each column and the space between them. The space between columns is known as a gutter. Remember that too many columns on a page will look fussy and will be irritating to read.

Page numbers

If a document has several pages, it is a good idea to number the pages. If the pages get out of order it is then easy to re-order them. It is also easy to see if a page is missing. Page numbers will be needed if the document is to include a table of contents.

Page numbers are usually incorporated into a header or footer in the form of a code which is automatically translated into page numbers when the document is printed. This means that the author does not need to number each page separately. Page numbers are usually displayed in the centre of a header or footer or in the top or bottom corner of each page. Figure 1.15 shows a document with the page number included in a footer.

Activity

Look at the software you use, how would you insert page numbers into the footer? Can you set the software to count the number of pages you create and insert that information, e.g. 'Page 1 of 30'.

Templates

When you design a document layout you will need to consider all the layout features listed above. If you are going to produce the same type of document again, you will want to save the layout so that you can use it again without having to set it all up each time. You can save document layouts as templates.

A template is a blank document that has all the layout information in it. It may also contain codes to prompt the user to type the correct information into the document in the right places. When a new document is created all the layout details and information from the template are 'copied' onto the new document. The user simply continues with the creation of the required document and does not have to keep remembering and applying these settings to each document. The manuscript which was the basis of this book was created using a template that had all the necessary settings, e.g. double spacing text, standard font settings and margin sizes, etc.

Activity

Some software comes with some templates already available. Look at the software you will use. What templates are there? Do you like them? Are they good styles?

Document contents

Documents are made up of three main types of data:

- Text
- Graphics
- Tables

Text

Text is usually entered via the keyboard or by importing another document into the one on which you are working. However, there is now software available that allows you to enter text to a document by other means. You may 'dictate' to the computer. While this is not as accurate for some as using the keyboard it is a method which is improving technically and for some of us may be much more accurate than our use of the keyboard.

Activity

Investigate this and see what you can find about the software. Many computing magazines have reviewed these applications. What were their views?

Graphics

Most people are familiar with the saying 'A picture is worth a thousand words'. Pictures and illustrations are very important to us. Take a simple example. One of your friends is giving you directions to their house. It's a complicated journey, and you become totally confused with the number of left and right turns and the descriptions of landmarks for which you should look. Therefore, you ask them to draw you a map. This makes the journey much simpler – you can see the route you will need to take. The map helps you to understand the information your friend is giving you.

Throughout your course, diagrams and illustrations will be used to help you to understand the concepts you are being taught. This book contains diagrams to explain the text.

Pictures and diagrams are essential in industry. Imagine trying to build a house without any plans!

Graphics are pictures and diagrams which are included in a document. They may be simple diagrams or more complex pictures such as clip art from a graphics package. A chart from a spreadsheet could be included as a graphic.

Tables

Tables may be created as part of word processing documents or they may be imported into documents from other packages such as spreadsheets.

Tables provide a useful way of presenting information that enables the reader to quickly identify the important points. There are tables used within this book to present information and you will use tables within some of your coursework.

Earlier we mentioned football league results and that the data is presented using tables. Imagine trying to present the same data in paragraphs of text.

Activity

How much text would be necessary? Would it be interesting? What sort of information do you think is most suitable for presentation in a table?

Editing text

Text which has been added to a document by typing at the keyboard or by being dictated or imported from another document can be edited and manipulated in many ways. Editing can range from simple correction of typing errors to major changes of layout. You should consult the user manuals for your package for details of the facilities available

Word processors operate in either insert or overtype mode. In insert mode, text is inserted at the cursor position. If you need to add text, you position the cursor where you want the text and then begin typing. The new text is inserted and the existing text is pushed along, automatically being reformatted. If the word processor is using overtype mode, the text you type overwrites the existing text. Most modern packages allow you to switch between the two modes. Make sure you know which mode you are using. It can be very annoying to lose work because you didn't realise you were using overtype mode!

Text can be deleted in a number of ways. In general, the backspace key deletes the character to its left and the delete key removes the character to its right. Text can usually be deleted by the process of highlighting the required text and then pressing the delete or backspace key. Another way of deleting text is to select it and then use the package's cut function to remove it.

When you use a cut function, the text you have cut is removed from the document and held in a temporary store. In many common applications, the cut text is

Organisation Chart for Wicker's World Ltd

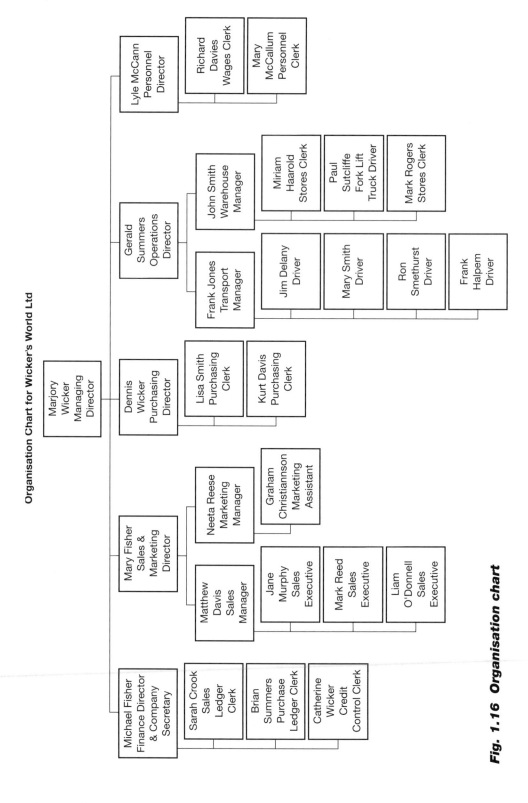

Fig. 1.16 Organisation chart

held in the clipboard. Cut text can be replaced in a document, or in another document, by means of the paste function. Cutting and pasting can be used to copy text to another part of the document or into another document and to move text to another part of a document.

Text can be enhanced by being made bold or italic or by being underlined. Highlighting should be used sparingly or its effect will be lost. Different type sizes can also be used to emphasise document and section headings.

Editing graphics

Graphics packages frequently combine features of both the painting and drawing packages. Drawing features allow shapes such as lines, circles and boxes to be used to create organisation charts, flow charts and simple technical diagrams. Figure 1.16 shows an organisation chart created using a business graphics package. Shapes can be filled with colour or patterns. Text can be added. Clip art images, usually in bitmap form, can be added to diagrams

Business graphics packages can be used to produce charts or graphs to display data, in a similar way to the graphs and charts produced by spreadsheet packages such as Microsoft® Excel and Lotus 1-2-3. A range of chart formats is available, including area, bar, line and pie charts and 3D versions of these forms.

Graphics will normally be prepared using an appropriate graphics package and then added to a document. It may be possible to use the cut and paste function to copy a graphic from the package in which it was produced or an entire graphics file may be included.

Most graphic design software packages include clip art – ready drawn graphics that you can include in your work. These images are stored in bitmap form, which means that the image is stored as a pattern of dots, or pixels. Therefore, changing the size of the image may affect the resolution (the clarity of the image). When a bitmap image is enlarged the detail often becomes 'fuzzy'.

Activity

Import a piece of clip art into a document. Now enlarge it by clicking on the image then clicking and dragging one of the 'handles'. What happens? Can you reduce it again? How far can you reduce it?

Explore the graphic components that are available for you to use with the software packages to which you have access.

Once a graphic has been included in a document it may need to be manipulated. For example, it may be necessary to adjust the size of the graphic to fit the document. Most word processing packages have facilities that allow you to alter the size, rotate, copy and move graphics within a document.

Editing tables

A table may simply consist of text arranged in columns and rows, as shown in the top part of Figure 1.17. This table was created by setting the appropriate tabs to align the text.

Item	Colour	Price
T-shirt	Red	£15.99
T-shirt	Green	£15.99
Socks	Grey	£4.99
Shorts	White	£17.99

Surname	First name	Age	Class
Brown	Jennifer	14	3C
Jones	David	12	2F
Smith	John	15	3C
Taylor	Brenda	16	4T

Fig. 1.17 Simple table created using tabs (top) and a more complex table created using a table facility (bottom)

However, modern word processing packages have a more powerful table function which allows the user to set up tables with varying numbers of rows and columns. It is then possible to manipulate the data in the table and the overall appearance of the table. The bottom part of Figure 1.17 shows a table that has been set up using such a facility.

The user is able to select the number of rows and columns required, to set the widths of the columns and the height of the rows. Borders, grid lines and shading can be added. Text can be entered into the cells of the table and then manipulated. In effect, each cell can be treated as a mini document and the text can be edited, highlighted and aligned as required.

Additional rows and columns can be added to the table if needed, and rows and columns can be removed.

Some packages allow the user to carry out simple arithmetic operations on data held in tables – similar to a spreadsheet. However, these functions will be limited compared to the power of a spreadsheet. If complex calculations were needed, it would be better to use a spreadsheet to create the table and then to insert the spreadsheet into the document.

Finding and combining data

Some documents will be created by combining data from a number of sources. For example, you might wish to include part of an existing document in the one you are preparing or you might want to add a graphic that has been produced using a graphics presentation package.

One way to include data is by cutting and pasting. Most word processing packages also have a facility that allows the user to find and include other documents or files. You will need to know where the file has been stored on the computer, i.e. you will need to know the directory it is stored in and the name of the file, including any file extension.

The file you wish to include must also be in an acceptable format. Many word processing packages can accept documents that have been produced using another word processor because they are able to convert the file formats. For example, Word is able to convert documents created using WordPerfect software. Graphics must be stored in an acceptable format if they are to be included in documents. You should consult the user manuals for your software to find which formats are acceptable.

Saving documents

After you have created your document you will need to save it. If you are going to save your documents on the hard drive of your computer, you will need to have created appropriate directories for your files. You should save your working files in separate directories to the word processing software so that there is no risk of confusing the files. You should also organise your directories in a way which will help you to find your files later. For example, you would probably find it useful to keep all documents that are part of your school or college work in a separate directory.

If you need to store your documents on a floppy drive, you will need to make sure that you have some formatted disks available to hold your documents.

You will need to give your documents appropriate filenames. These must be valid filenames on your system. For example, if you are using a machine that uses Microsoft Windows® 3.1, your filenames must not exceed eight characters, as this is the limit imposed by the DOS operating system. However, if you are using Microsoft® Windows 95 and later you can use up to 30 characters and employ spaces. You will need to check what is acceptable as a filename on the system you are using. Remember that if it is important to be able to move a file between different machines, you must use a convention with which they can all cope. If you are using a machine with Microsoft® Windows 95 operating system and need to transfer a file to another using Microsoft® Windows 3.1 it is wise to only use eight character filenames. You will also need to check if it is necessary to add a file extension after your filename – most packages do this automatically for you.

The filenames you choose must also be meaningful to you. Give your documents names that you will recognise. If you don't, you will waste a lot of time searching for the documents you want to use!

Standard ways of working

There are many areas in an organisation that require a standard approach. For example, letters issued by any organisation, from any department, should be identifiable as from that organisation.

Information technology makes it very easy for information to be lost or misused, either accidentally or maliciously. All users need to be aware of the following dangers:

- Original work may be copied by an unauthorised person who then presents it as their own. How will you secure your work?
- Unauthorised people may access confidential material. How might a doctor secure their patient records?
- A virus may damage data or other files. How might this be prevented?

- Computers may be damaged making it impossible to recover data. What would you do to ensure that if a computer is damaged the data is not lost?
- Readers may be confused or annoyed by inaccurate or poorly written material. In the documents you have collected can you find such an example?
- Professionally presented information may be believed, even if incorrect. Can you remember any statements made by newspapers that later they had to apologise for?
- IT operators may be subjected to unnecessary hazards or stress due to poorly laid out workplaces. Do you sit comfortably?

You are expected to use techniques to ensure a consistency of appearance in all your GNVQ work. You must be sure to:

- Manage your work effectively
- Keep your information secure
- Produce accurate and readable information
- Use commonly acceptable standards
- Work safely

One method that might be employed to help achieve standard ways of working is to use macros.

Macros

Macros can be used in many ways in word processing and spreadsheet packages. Some common uses of macros are:

- To store regularly used keystroke sequences
- To produce documents with standard formats
- To set defaults
- To carry out simple calculations

Let's look at some of these uses of macros in more detail.

Storing keystrokes

The simple save and print macro is an example of a macro that is used to automate a procedure that is likely to be needed on a regular basis. Without the macro, the user of the package will need to enter the instructions step by step. If the save and print macro is assigned to a key or an icon, it can be called up quickly – removing the need to enter the same commands each time.

Entering a sequence of commands or keystrokes that is needed regularly is a very common use of macros. The save and print macro stores commands. An example of a macro that could be used to enter a sequence of keystrokes is one you could create to a type your name in a document. Once you have set it up, it will obviously be quicker to use the macro rather than to type your name letter by letter.

Activity

How would you create this macro?

This type of macro is also very useful if you need to insert special characters into a document. Many keyboards do not have keys for symbols such as ǧ or š. If you need to use one of these symbols, you will have to select it from a symbol set. You can speed up your work by writing a macro that inserts the required character when you press an appropriate key combination.

You will sometimes find yourself needing to insert larger amounts of text into documents – whole paragraphs or, indeed, several paragraphs. You could store the text in a macro, it would be quicker to let the macro key the text, rather than type it yourself each time. However, this would not be the best way to handle this task. Some packages restrict the amount of text you can store in a macro, so you might not be able to include all the text needed. Another point to consider is what will happen if the standard text changes. If you have stored the text in a macro you will probably have to rerecord the macro to take account of the changes. A more efficient method of inserting a larger amount of text into documents is to store the standard text as a separate document and then to write a macro that calls up the required document and inserts it into the document at the point where it is needed. Then, if the standard text changes, you only have to edit the document holding this text; the macro can be left alone.

Standard formats

An important use of macros in applications packages is in the production of documents with standard formats.

Have another look at the layout of a business letter (see Figure 1.2, page 8). You could consider the letter as being made up of three main parts:

- Formatting information such as the paper size, margins and text fonts
- Fixed text such as the company's address
- Variable text such as the recipient's name and address, the date and the main text of the letter

Macros find many applications in spreadsheet packages. As in the case of word processing packages, macros in spreadsheets can be used:

- To store regularly used keystroke sequences
- To produce documents with standard formats
- To set defaults
- To carry out calculations

Macros can be used to store text strings such as your name that you might want to insert into a spreadsheet. The amount of text you can store in this way is generally much less than you can store in a word processing macro.

You can also create macros that hold the commands needed for tasks you carry out regularly, such as the save and print routine mentioned earlier.

Another task where this sort of macro can be very useful is in the creation of charts. Suppose that you have created a spreadsheet showing sales figures. From time to time, you need to produce a chart using these figures. There are a number of steps involved in producing a chart, so if you save them into a macro, you will be able to run the macro and quickly produce the chart whenever you wish.

Activity

How could you use a macro to help you produce a letter with a standard layout like the one in Figure 1.2 on page 8?

You could record a macro containing all the keystrokes and commands needed to set the basic format of the letter and to type in the fixed text. A macro like this would deal with the standard part of the letter. But would this be the best method? As was pointed out in the previous section, if you store large amounts of information in a macro, you can have problems if any parts of the information change. If you need to change some of the details, such as the margins or part of the address, you would probably find yourself rerecording the macro to make these changes.

A better approach would be to use a template document to hold the standard information for the letter. A simple template document might just contain the formatting information and the company's address. This document could be stored and called up each time you needed to type a letter. You could even write a macro to open the template document for you.

Templates are very powerful word processing tools and you could make your letter template far more useful than the simple one described above. It is possible to embed codes in template documents to set the positions of variable text and to prompt for the input of that text. Therefore, in your letter template, you could include codes to set the positions where the recipient's name and address are to be typed. Another useful code to include is a date code, which will automatically include the current date in your letter. The use of this template could then be combined with a macro that would open the template document and prompt you for the information needed at each code position.

Activity

Suppose you often need to include standard paragraphs in the letters you produce. How could you do this?

You could store the standard paragraphs as individual documents and then write macros to retrieve the appropriate document and insert it into your letter. You could write a macro that would pause at the point where the standard text is needed and display a list of the available paragraphs so that you can select the one you want.

Activity

Can you think of other possible uses for templates and macros?

Just as you can use templates and macros in word processing to create standard documents, you can use them in spreadsheets to produce worksheets with standard layouts.

2000 MONTHLY SALES FIGURES

	Region 1	Region 2	Region 3	Total sales	
Jan	£1,000.00	£1,203.00	£1,699.00	**£3,902.00**	
Feb	£768.00	£567.00	£457.00	**£1,792.00**	
Mar	£646.00	£234.00	£678.00	**£1,558.00**	
Apr	£1,289.00	£780.00	£987.00	**£3,056.00**	
May	£590.00	£450.00	£1,200.00	**£2,240.00**	
Jun	£2,009.00	£300.00	£300.00	**£2,609.00**	— June total
Jul	£743.00	£653.00	£789.00	**£2,185.00**	
Aug	£859.00	£790.00	£456.00	**£2,105.00**	
Sep	£1,002.00	£1,473.00	£976.00	**£3,451.00**	
Oct	£880.00	£876.00	£340.00	**£2,096.00**	
Nov	£1,356.00	£1,287.00	£1,598.00	**£4,241.00**	
Dec	£2,003.00	£3,006.00	£3,100.00	**£8,109.00**	
Totals	**£13,145.00**	**£11,619.00**	**£12,580.00**	**£37,344.00**	

Region 2 total

Fig. 1.18 A spreadsheet table showing sales figures

Look at the worksheet shown in Figure 1.18. If you were to create a worksheet that contained the title information, the row and column labels and the formulae needed to produce the total figures, you could save this as a template. You could recall this template whenever you needed it and type in the variable information (i.e. the actual figures). You could use a macro to open the template and prompt the user to enter the required information.

Templates can be used whenever you need to produce standard documents – letters, address labels, invoices, minutes of meetings and reports. You do not have to write macros to make use of templates, but together they are a very powerful combination.

Setting defaults

Macros can be a useful way of setting up an applications package to work in the way you want.

Suppose you normally work with the unit of measurement set to inches. This will mean that margins, tab positions, indents, column spacing etc. will be measured and displayed in inches. However, for some documents you need to work in centimetres. A macro is a very convenient way to change this default. If you write one macro to set the unit of measurement to centimetres and another to set it back to inches, you can switch between the two systems very easily.

Another default setting you might change with a macro is print settings. Suppose your computer is linked to two printers. One of these is a dot matrix printer that is used for draft printing and you print working copies of documents on this printer. However, when you are ready to print out a final copy of a document, you need to redirect the document to a laser printer that produces higher quality output. A macro that selects the laser printer when you need it will save you time.

You can also use macros to change the way documents are displayed on the screen and the default folder used to save documents.

Spreadsheet defaults may be set using macros in the same way as for word processing packages.

Calculations

Some word processing packages allow you to carry out simple calculations. While the facilities available in a word processor are not as powerful as those you will find in a spreadsheet package, they can still be quite useful. For example, you may be able to set up a table and use the maths facility to calculate the totals.

In a word processing package, the calculated figures are not automatically recalculated if a figure in the table is changed, as would be the case with a spreadsheet package. If you alter any of the figures, you need to recalculate any related figures.

If you found that you often needed to use a similar table in a letter or document, you could store the table layout in the document template and create a macro that would prompt you for the table entries and then update the calculated figures for you.

Spreadsheet packages are designed to handle numbers and there are a wide range of functions to carry out calculations. In many spreadsheet applications, you will use formulae entered onto the worksheet to carry out the calculations. The spreadsheet shown in Figure 1.18 has been set up in this way – as you enter the monthly figures, the total sales are calculated.

There might be occasions when you want to carry out some calculations on the figures in the spreadsheet. You don't want the results to be displayed all the time. For example, you might want to calculate the maximum, minimum and average sales values for each region from time to time and only display the figures when you need them.

You could do this by creating a macro that finds the maximum and minimum figures, calculates the average for each region, and then adds them to the spreadsheets, with appropriate labels. When you have finished with the figures, you can delete them and use the macro to calculate them again when you need them.

Organisations and standard formats

The standard formats employed by organisations will govern many aspects of the organisation and include:

- How documents are presented
- How data is stored
- Who may access certain data
- How customers are treated

Some of this is necessary in order for the organisation to comply with the law.

Security procedures

All organisations take steps to protect the data that is held in their computer systems as it represents a valuable resource to them.

Computer systems need to be protected against **theft**. Hardware and software are expensive and most organisations will take steps to protect it in the same way as they protect their other assets and property.

The contents of documents may be confidential and must be protected against **unauthorised access**. Systems and documents can be protected by passwords. Source documents and printed copies of documents should not be left lying around – they should be locked away when they are not being used. Employees also have a responsibility not to divulge confidential information. Data may also be copyright material. The software you are using certainly is and should not be copied except for backup purposes.

While you are working on a document it should be saved regularly. Remember, if the computer fails or is switched off, any data stored in the computer's **random access memory (RAM)** will be lost. It is a good idea to get into the habit of saving work in progress every few minutes. Then if disaster does strike, you won't lose too much. If your software allows automatic saving at intervals it is worth using this option.

You should also **back up** your files and documents. This means taking a copy, probably on floppy disk, and storing it away from the computer. Then, if the copy of a document on the computer's hard drive or your working floppy disk becomes damaged or corrupted, or if you accidentally delete or overwrite a document, you will have another copy of your document to which you can go back. You should back up your files regularly – at least at the end of each working day.

Source documents should be kept until they can be replaced with a printed copy of the word processed document. Then, if all the versions on the computer should be lost, the document can be retyped.

One of the potentially destructive events that can cause loss of data or even the corruption of software is the introduction to the system of a **virus**. A computer virus is a rogue program that is written specifically to destroy. These programs may be introduced maliciously by an individual or group intending damage, or even accidentally. Many organisations have regulations in place to try to limit the chances of this occurring. It may be that machines are not fitted with a floppy drive, so removing the simplest method of infection. Some organisations state that no unauthorised software is to be loaded onto company hardware. This should prevent accidental infection.

However, it is not wise to rely on these physical methods to prevent infection. A virus may enter a system with a legitimate document, perhaps an e-mail from a customer. To combat this most systems use another program that checks for viruses and 'cleans up' the infection.

Activity

Investigate the names and costs of the popular anti-virus programs.

Working safely

Most of the means by which you can ensure you work safely are common sense. Sometimes, because we are familiar with an environment, we become careless.

For example, it is easy to put a cup of coffee or an open can of cola next to the computer while we work. We may start out being careful not to knock it over.

However all too easily we become distracted or absorbed in what we are doing. We reach for the mouse and knock the drink over the keyboard and desk.

Many thousands of days work are lost in Britain due to back injuries. It is important therefore that we take care of how we sit at the keyboard and for how long. We need to consider the height of the chair and desk, how long we spend in front of the monitor, and how it is set. Is there any glare on the screen? Is it far enough away from us? Is the image clear and flicker free? For some people periods of time in front of incorrectly set monitors triggers epileptic fits or migraines. For most of us such conditions may prompt headaches and general discomfort.

We need to rest and change activities through the day to help us to avoid the many types of injuries associated with working at a computer.

The Health and Safety Executive publish information leaflets that identify the layout we should adopt when sitting at our computers. We are also advised to get up and move around at regular intervals to prevent muscular stiffness, as this can lead to injury.

The time spent staring at a computer screen should be broken up. Our eyes need exercise too! We should look away from the screen and focus on distant objects to keep our eye-muscles working and fit. This helps prevent eye strain. The monitor settings should be adjusted depending upon the surrounding light levels and our personal preferences. Screens that are too bright or too dull cause strain as we try to see them. Screens should be placed at eye level to enable us to use them easily.

Correct lighting is very inportant. Screens should not be placed in the path of direct light, for example a window with bright sunshine streaming in. The best lighting, is that you don't notice.

Cables must not be allowed to trail across the floor or under desks as trailing cables pose a trip hazard. They must be suitably insulated to avoid shocks or fires being caused.

Activity

Look around the area in which you work. What hazards are there of which you need to be aware? What changes would you recommend to improve the safety of yourself and others?

Assessment evidence

For you to be successful in your external assessment you will need to provide evidence that you understand the different purposes for which documents are produced. You will include:

- A range of writing styles and layouts
- Some text created by you as well as some collected from other sources
- Tables containing structured information
- Graphics, such as pictures, drawings or clip art

Your tutor will guide you in preparing for the assessment. By using all your skills you may be able to achieve a higher grade.

To help you improve your grade read the information given in Figure 1.19.

To achieve a pass you must ensure that you can do all the parts mentioned in the pass column.

Can you use an appropriate writing style? Do you know the difference between formal and informal written language? Do you know how the different layouts help you project an image?

Can you use each of the following effectively and appropriately?

- Page orientation
- Paragraph formats
- Line spacing
- Headings
- Margins
- Headers and footers
- Tabs (tabulations)
- Bullets
- Fonts
- Borders and shading

You must be able to create and arrange suitable information, showing that you can use

- Text
- Pictures
- Drawings
- Charts
- Tables

Are you careful and accurate in your work? Do you always keep backup copies of files in case of accident?

Are you able to clearly describe and compare different layouts used by others? Can you compare documents produced by other organisations with your own? Can you identify similarities and differences between your documents and those of other organisations?

If you can do all this then you should now look at the merit column in Figure 1.19. Once you are confident in your ability to achieve this and with the guidance of your tutor to help you improve you should then look to the column headed distinction.

Pass	Merit	Distinction
To achieve a pass your work must show:	To achieve a merit your work must show:	To achieve a distinction your work must show:
• Your ability to choose and use appropriate writing styles and layouts so that your documents work as intended.	• Imaginative use of document layouts and presentation techniques to achieve good quality and an appropriate impact in your documents.	• Different types of information organised into a convincing and coherent presentation.
• Appropriate use of page orientation, paragraph formats, line spacing, headings, margins, header/footers, tabs, bullets, fonts, borders and shading to enhance your documents.	• Your ability to proof-read your work and correct obvious errors.	• Information that is accurate and concise and presented in ways that make it easy to understand.
• Your ability to originate suitable information and combine appropriately with different types of material selected from other sources to create combinations of text, pictures, drawings, charts and tables.	• Relevant explanations for the differences between each of the documents used by different organisations and your own documents.	• Your ability to use technical language fluently and produce clear, coherent and comprehensive explanations and annotations.
• Your ability to check the accuracy of your work and keep backup copies of your files.	• Your ability to work independently to produce your work to agreed deadlines.	• A constructive evaluation of your documents that identifies good and less good features, suggests possible improvements to them and compares them with standards used by organisations.
• A clear description and comparison of different layouts, identifying similarities and differences.	• Your ability to save and annotate draft work to show clearly the development process for two of your documents.	

Fig. 1.19 Unit 1 Presenting Information – grade descriptors

Unit 2

HANDLING INFORMATION

Introduction

What is information?

Classifying information

Developing and presenting information

Databases

Spreadsheets

Organisations and their use of information

Security procedures

Assessment evidence

Introduction

In this unit you will learn how to manage information. You will learn different ways to process information before it is presented. This unit may be taught together with Unit 1, Presenting information.

In creating documents there are a number of computerised tools available to you. These involve the use of various software applications.

During your studies you will learn to produce a database and a spreadsheet. You will learn about how an organisation handles information by using databases and spreadsheets. You may use the information you handle in this unit to create the documents you need as evidence for Unit 1, Presenting information.

The topics you will cover in this unit include:

- What is information?
- Classifying information
- Developing and presenting information
- Databases
- Spreadsheets
- Organisations and their use of information
- Security procedures

What is information?

One could define information in many ways. In reality it consists of small items, called data. This data is then manipulated to give us information.

Data is the term used to refer to facts that require processing to produce useful information. For example consider this list:

- 05/02/76
- 23/09/71
- 12/12/78
- 30/07/77

It is not particularly useful. You may be able to see that they are all dates, but so what? What is their significance? These are items of data.

Let's look at another list:

- Sîan
- Neeta
- Mark
- Roger

Just a list of names, more data.

Now manipulate the two lists of data, suppose we say that item one in the list of dates, 05/02/76, goes with Sîan, and item two in the list with Neeta, and so on. We now have a list of dates and names. This is still data until you know the relationship between each item. As soon as we know that the dates are in fact, the dates of birth of the individuals listed, it becomes information that is useful.

Consider this list:

- 516 6547
- 518 9826
- 515 6791
- 678 9512
- David Donaldson
- Hilary Hines
- Jane Jones
- Michael Merchant

This is another list of fairly meaningless data. You may decide from the layout that they are telephone numbers, but whose?

Now we process the data to give us Table 2.1. We can now see to whom each number belongs. Therefore we can say that information is the result of manipulating data into a useful format.

Table 2.1 Directors' telephone numbers

Director Name	Emergency Contact Number
David Donaldson	518 9826
Hilary Hines	678 9512
Jane Jones	516 6547
Michael Merchant	515 6791

We store and manipulate data in many different ways. Each of the items above, comprising the director name and contact number, is called a **record**. The parts of the record, e.g. the director name, are called **fields**. In the example there are four records, each of which consists of two fields.

Record structures

Data handling systems are widely used in many organisations, and by individuals. Many of you may well use such a system yourselves. How many of you keep address books? Or a note of friends' and relatives' birthdays? These are paper based data storage systems; they enable you to retrieve the information you need, when you need it. Now wouldn't it be useful if the birthday book could select an address and send the appropriate birthday card to arrive on the birthday?

Other data handling may be done by simply grouping together an amount of text into one document, for example a letter. Normally when talking of data handling and the structure of such data we look to databases and the file structures they are based upon. These use data storage in such a way as to enable the rapid recall of data and the manipulation of the same data into a variety of useful presentations.

Databases use many terms that have historically been applied to paperwork that stores information. Consider an insurance broker. The broker makes a profit by selling various insurance policies to clients. The broker will earn commission from the insurance company on the policies sold. To maximise business the broker keeps files containing various details of each client. Before databases were so widely employed the broker may have kept such details in files of cards, one for each client. A representation of such a card is shown in Figure 2.1.

Activity

What other item of data do you think might be included on this card?

We have detailed here the name and address of the client together with his telephone number. Also there is a **data item** called the client number. This item enables the broker to identify a particular client. This is because there may be more than one client with this name. This data item is known as the **key field** and is unique to the record. In this example there is only need for the client number to identify the record, and it is therefore described as the **primary key**. If the broker did not have the client number to use as the primary key, they may choose to use a combination of fields to identify the record. The broker might choose to use the surname combined with the date of birth to identify the particular client. This gives us the date of birth as the **secondary key**.

Remember this card is one of many. The collection of cards together is known as a **file**. Within any file are a number of records. The example card shown in Figure 2.1 is one **record**. It contains details of one individual whereas the file contains the details of many individuals.

A stock file will contain information about all stock and a stock record contains the details of one type of stock. For example, in a commercial garage it might be about a particular size and type of tyre.

Activity

Can you think of any other files? What information might they contain?

Surname	Forename(s)		Client number
Jones	Matthew Thomas		99-4625
Address	32 Devises Crescent		
	Anothertown		
	Anyshire		
Postcode	AA2 2P2		
Telephone	0123-789-9512		

Fig. 2.1 Representation of a file card

Each record in the file consists of a collection of data items. In the example given these are:

- Surname
- Forename(s)
- Address
- Postcode
- Telephone number
- Client number

Each of these pieces of information is known as a **field**. As can be seen in this example each field has a **name**, as in this case the field name will usually describe the contents. In the example above would it be of any use for each field to be numbered thus?

- 1
- 2
- 3
- 4
- 5
- 6

Obviously not. The various fields contain different data. The field containing surname needs less space than that containing the address, so they will be of different lengths.

Structuring the data in this way enables the easy manipulation of the data, either in the presentation of data to the user or to perform some task. Such a task might be the comparison of individual items of data within a series of records. Consider the following:

Manchester Utd, Arsenal, Liverpool, Chelsea, Blackburn Rovers, Derby County, Leicester City, Leeds Utd, West Ham Utd, Coventry City, Southampton, Sheffield Wednesday, Wimbledon, Aston Villa, Everton, Tottenham Hotspur, Bolton Wanderers, Crystal Palace, Barnsley, Manchester City, 0, 0, 0, 0, 1, 0, 0, 1, 0, 2, 0, 1, 1, 0, etc.

What on earth is it? The structure of the data doesn't help you at all. The enthusiasts among you will have recognised the names of a series of professional football teams. However, the data is still meaningless. Now we shall structure it and give names to the fields as seen in Table 2.2.

Table 2.2 Football results table

Team	Games played	Away draws	Home draws	Home wins	Away wins
Manchester Utd	0	0	0	0	0
Arsenal	1	0	0	1	0
Liverpool	2	1	0	1	0
Chelsea	2	0	1	1	0

We can see that collecting the data together is of no earthly use unless it is formatted and presented in a useful manner.

One of the most familiar record structures is that used in the telephone directory.

Activity

Look in your local directory and identify the individual records of data. What names might be used to refer to the fields within each record?

Many of you will be familiar with the large mail order catalogues that have been operating for many years. Initially goods were delivered to customers after a written order had been received. Nowadays, although this service is still available, increasingly orders are accepted over the telephone.

The customer registers with the company who issues them with a unique identifying number. This is used as an account number. When the customer wishes to purchase goods they telephone in an order. This order will consist of certain data items. These are:

- Customer number
- Customer name
- Customer address
- Catalogue number (unique to each item type)
- Item description
- Colour/size required
- Quantity required
- Item price

This could be said to be the structure of the order.

The structure of the file that records the movements of stock will contain some fields in common with those used in the order file. These are:

- Item number (unique to the item, called catalogue number in the example above)
- Item description
- Item price

Other fields are needed in the stock record, for example, number in stock, reorder level and perhaps a supplier's code.

Activity

Are there any other fields you can think of that might be included?

When we visit a doctor our 'records' are extracted from file. These record various details that are required by the doctor during the consultation and treatment. The details stored in these records include:

- NHS number (this is unique to each individual)
- Name of patient
- Address of patient
- Date of birth
- Dates of visits
- Diagnosis
- Treatment

A walk along almost any high street will take you past an estate agent. Consider the information they need. They will keep data on the properties on their books for sale, for example:

- Type of property (detached, semi-detached, flat, bungalow, etc.)
- Number of bedrooms
- Number of reception rooms
- Whether or not central heating is installed

Much more data will be needed than listed above – add to these yourself.

There will be files for the current owners of the properties and those who are interested in buying.

Activity

What data will be needed for each group of people?

Number structures

It is not always useful to store data in the types of record structures we have seen above. Some data needs to be used in calculations or in decision making. In the decision-making process the data may be further processed and analysed. This is frequently the case with numerical data such as financial information.

In weather forecasting, numerical data is used to predict weather patterns. This data is taken from a variety of sources such as satellites and weather stations and compared with previously collected and analysed data in order to predict the future pattern.

Another example of numerical structure might include that shown in Table 2.3.

Table 2.3 2000 monthly sales figures

2000 MONTHLY SALES FIGURES (£)	Region 1	Region 2	Region 3
January	1,000.00	1,203.00	1,699.00
February	768.00	567.00	457.00
March	646.00	234.00	678.00
April	1,289.00	780.00	987.00
May	590.00	450.00	1,200.00
June	2,009.00	300.00	300.00
July	743.00	653.00	789.00
August	859.00	790.00	456.00
September	1,002.00	1,473.00	976.00
October	880.00	876.00	340.00
November	1,356.00	1,287.00	1,598.00
December	2,003.00	3,006.00	3,100.00
Totals	£13,145.00	£11,619.00	£12,580.00

We can see here the two-dimensional view of data presented in a table. The data may be grouped according to the region or by the month. This data can be used to project future sales.

We might have data that relates to the income and expenditure of an organisation or individual. This sort of financial information is commonly used to project future trends, estimate cash needs and determine profit or loss.

Great Britain has the largest proportion of homeowners in the world. According to the *Housing Statistics Summary No. 6, 2000* 69 per cent of British households are occupied by the owners. This has been achieved by the mortgage system. A mortgage is a loan taken out using the house as security, i.e. if the loan is not repaid then the loan company may take possession of the house and sell it to recover the debt. For many people this is the largest debt they will ever have and they need to know how much the repayments will be to enable them decide whether they can afford to buy. To help them in this process the loan company will give a table of repayments that will quote for the possible rates of interest.

The statement made above about the proportion of homeowners in the population is based upon government statistics (more data are available on the sites www.open.gov.uk and www.detr.gov.uk). Statistics are a mathematical generalisation based upon real figures. These are often presented in the form of a table, as seen above with the sales figures. Comparisons are made against other countries based upon numbers of population and the percentage of that population. You will frequently find statistical information presented in tabular form.

Finding information

We have talked above about how information might be presented. However, information needs to be found before it can be presented. Sources vary depending upon the information required and resources available.

During your studies you will have to find information that you need. Perhaps you are asked to research current computer prices. Where would you look for the information? Whom could you ask? Would you go to the library? In what types of books might you find the information? You will need to use a variety of different methods to find your information.

Would you use the computer to search databases? If so, which would you use? You might choose to search the Internet for the information. What words would you use to search? Would the television or the radio provide useful information? Are newspapers likely to contain such information?

There are many questions to be asked when researching for useful information.

The most important thing to remember when using information sources is to consider the integrity of the source that you access. How reliable and accurate is it? If you do not require reliable and accurate information then this is of little importance. However, much of the information you will seek in your course will need to be validated and verified.

Validation is confirming how likely it is that the information is correct. For example, you will know that if a date of birth is given as 30 February it is not going to be correct.

To **verify** the integrity of any data you will need to consider the source, is it one in which you have trust? If not then perhaps you will need to cross-check using other sources. To be sure of using the most accurate information all information should be cross-checked with other sources.

People as sources

Your first information source is talking to people who have extensive knowledge about the subject which you wish to know about. For example, should you wish to know about the performance record of a particular football team, you might contact the supporters club.

If you are asked to design a new document to be used in an office you would need to be able to talk to the people who will use this document.

- What does it need to say?
- In what order should information be presented on it?
- In what format does the document need to be, paper or electronic?

The questions asked must be appropriate to the position of the people being questioned. If you need to know on what day the most post is handled in an organisation you should ask the administration staff who handle it and not the Managing Director. In different circumstances and with different needs these questions will change.

When you are organising a party or a night out with friends you speak to them to find out information, for example:

- Are they interested in the party?
- Are they able to come?
- Who will come?
- What time will you meet?
- Where will you meet?

And many more. People are an important source of data or information depending on circumstances.

Consider earlier, when we were talking about finding information, we mentioned using a library. We might make a decision as to whether or not to do so after asking the opinion of the librarian. The librarian in a modern library will also be able to suggest suitable computer databases, they may be able to help you effectively search the Internet. The librarian has a role in helping you to find the information you need for the purposes you need it.

Books as sources

We talked above of using librarians as sources of information, to help you find other sources. One of the sources a librarian may point you to are the books within the library. Perhaps a section of the library contains a number of books that may be useful to you. There may be a specific book for which you are looking and the librarian will be able to help you locate it. You are currently using this book as a source of information.

As well as asking the librarian you will need to learn to use the catalogue system of the library. Most libraries use the same system and you will find books listed in the catalogue in two ways. The books will be listed by title alphabetically. They will also be listed alphabetically by author.

The library

Activity

Try looking up this book in the library. If you can't find it ask the librarian for help.

There are many types of books that you may use to provide information that will be useful to you, both during this course and in other areas of your life.

When you are looking for information in books, the title may assist you in identifying whether a particular book is likely to be helpful. Then to further satisfy yourself that a book is going to be useful you will look in the table of contents, where the chapter titles may give an indication of the subject matter. Another way of finding useful information from books is to use the index at the back. This lists various individual items that are mentioned in the text.

You may have used the table of contents in this book to help you find the information you need for your course. To find more specific information you may use the index to identify the page number(s) on which the item is mentioned.

Books will usually contain information of a general or more lasting kind; for example there are many books about geography. The landmasses of the earth change so slowly that a book may contain relevant information many years after it was written.

Other books, however, will date. The book you are reading now is the result of the GNVQ syllabus changing and so a new text was needed.

Many books contain opinions and so you may choose to read a number of books on a particular topic to give a more balanced view. An example might be philosophy, or the fortunes of a particular football team.

Computer databases

Many computer databases contain information that will be useful to you. The library you use may have all their books catalogued using a computer database rather than the individual index cards that used to be employed. This is an example of a record structured database.

These forms of data storage will require you to learn to use the sort and search facilities that are required to organise the information contained.

Consider this book. You want to find it at your library. You may remember that it has the phrase, 'information and communications technology' in the title and that 'Cross' was an author. You will use this to search the database.

You may search for 'information technology'. Having got a list of different books up you may need to sort them by author to find this particular book.

Activity

Try this. Is there any other search you might use to find the book?

You may sort the list you have found into alphabetical order, using one field, perhaps the name of the author. This could help you find other books that may help you. Is there any other field on which you might sort data? How many ways might the information be sorted?

Activity

Look for other examples of databases available to you and try these techniques on them. Use the help facilities to assist you in the searching and sorting.

If the data is numeric, perhaps financial information, then it may be stored using a spreadsheet. Spreadsheets are applications packages which are used to process numerical data. Examples of this type of software are Microsoft® Excel, Lotus 1-2-3, Quattro Pro and SuperCalc. Spreadsheet facilities are also included in integrated packages such as MS Works and WordPerfect Works. Spreadsheets are used in business, science, engineering, geography – in fact, in any subject area where there is a need to process numerical data.

A spreadsheet can be described as an electronic sheet of paper on which you can carry out calculations.

The basic layout of a spreadsheet is a table with vertical **columns** and horizontal **rows**. The columns are labelled with letters across the top of the table and the rows

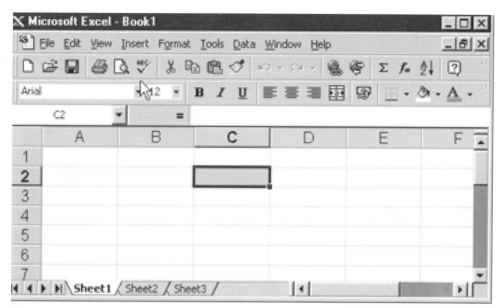

Fig. 2.2 A spreadsheet

with numbers down the left-hand side. The intersection of a row and a column is known as a **cell**. In Figure 2.2, the shaded cell is in row 2 and column C. It is therefore given the **cell address** or **cell reference** of C2. Every cell in a spreadsheet has a unique cell reference.

Figure 2.2 shows only a small part of a spreadsheet. An Excel spreadsheet, for example, can have 256 columns and 65,536 rows, but obviously you can't display it all on a computer screen at once.

The Internet as a source

The searching you did on the databases above will be valuable when you access the Internet. The volume of data available on the Internet is enormous and far more than may be contained in any one library.

When you search you should try to use an appropriate search 'engine'. Will it search UK only databases or US ones as well? Will it search the whole world?

Activity

Look at the search engines available to you? Is there more than one? What are they called? Where do they predominantly operate?

You may find that if you enter a simple word or phrase that there are too many '**hits**' returned to help you. A hit is where the search engine found your input word or phrase. If that is the case you will need to consider how you might 'refine' your search. This means that you will search your 'hits' for something a little more specific.

Having found the subject about which you are interested then you may read on and find that a word or phrase is interesting. If this item is in blue type with a solid underline then you have what is known as a '<u>hypertext</u>' link to further information as indicated by the word or phrase. If you click on that word then you will be taken to either another position in the current site or another site.

Having read the relevant article you may either return to the original page by using the 'back' button at the top of your screen or you may find another interesting link and follow that.

Television and radio

Television and radio are widely accepted as information providers. There are many educational and factual programmes broadcast. You may have watched some of the schools programmes on television at school, or perhaps listened to performances on radio that linked to your school studies.

You may not have noticed other programmes. For example, many Open University subjects are broadcast in the early hours of the morning. These programmes are advertised in the television schedules with the expectation that viewers will record the show to view later at a more convenient time.

Activity

Look in a TV listing guide. What programmes are listed? Could any be useful to your studies?

Person watching TV

Open university programmes are broadcast with education and formal courses in mind but there are many other programmes broadcast with a view to informing us. For instance, news programmes let us know what is happening in the various areas of the world. In current affairs programmes presenters tell us what is happening and perhaps some guests who have expertise in the field discuss the occurrences and speculate on the outcomes. There are also programmes that inform us of our legal rights and responsibilities.

Activity

List the programmes on television and radio that you are aware of and how they aim to inform us. Using the TV and radio schedules add to this with other programmes. Try watching and listening to programmes with which you are unfamiliar.

How would you decide upon the validity and verify the information given in these programmes?

Newspapers

Various national newspapers provide us with a daily diet of information. Some we may feel is useful and some not. There may be articles on current affairs and news reports. There may be feature articles, which give information on a particular subject that may not feature in either the news or current affairs articles.

Newspapers have different interests and you may choose to read the one that most closely matches your own views. Most newspapers are said to be of a particular political leaning. Many of us choose a newspaper because it is the one that our parents read, and so we are familiar with it.

Activity

Which newspaper do you prefer? Survey your friends and relatives and see which they prefer. How do the figures you come up with compare to the figures published by the papers?

The sales figures are usually published in the newspaper once a week or on their Internet sites.

Again, there are methods that we may use to validate the information given in newspapers. Is the report likely to be true? As little as ten years ago a cloned piglet would be seen as nonsense, today we accept it as likely to be true. We see the report published in a variety of places, including sources we trust. Therefore, short of contacting the individuals concerned directly, we accept the report as true. We consider it verified.

Timetables

These are a valuable source of factual information that is reasonably accurate. Let us suppose you wish to travel from Land's End to John o'Groats by train. Having mapped out a suitable rail route you will need to know the train times.

You will refer to a train timetable. Alternatively, you may phone the railway information centre where the operator will access the timetable for you and tell you the appropriate train times. You will start by stating the day or date on which you wish to travel. Then you will consider what time of day you want to start your journey. Perhaps you have a particular time at which you want to arrive. For the setting out time you will check to see what time the train is due to depart and for the arrival you will work back from the nearest arrival time that suits you.

If you decide to make the journey by bus there are many different timetables you will need to cover the journey.

Activity

Let us suppose you want to travel on 'The Blue Train' in South Africa. How do you find out the dates and times of travel? Where would you look for the information?

You might try the Internet or a travel agent. Which appeals to you? Which is likely to be accurate? How will you validate and verify the information you collect?

Compact disk (CD)

As well as a good source of music, compact disks are used to store electronic data in the form of software or databases of useful information. Many of you will have used and make use of these in your data collection. It is possible to hold the whole *Encyclopaedia Britannica* on CD. Many libraries stock back copies of the major news-

CD with message 'Teach yourself how to use the computer'

papers on CD, you may even buy them yourself. They are a valuable source of information and may be more easily indexed than the actual paper copies.

Activity

Which other encyclopaedia can you find stored on CD? How much data can be stored on CD?

There are many advantages to using CDs, including that it saves space in storage. They are also cheaper to produce than a book.

Items of interest may be linked to other items within the encyclopaedia by using the hypertext links referred to on page 60.

Personal notes

When you are working in class you will take notes during your lessons. These will often be invaluable to you, as they will cover the material in a manner which is more easily understood than the more formal handouts or textbooks you will read.

When you are searching for information useful to your course work you should make notes. These notes will include items of data about which you are interested and the sources from which you collected them.

Instruction manuals

During your course there are many opportunities for you to use software applications with which you are not very familiar. To do this you may use notes supplied by your tutor. However, you may find you want more information than is available to you from course notes so you may use the 'help' facilities.

These are a number of pages of information that you access by selecting search and inputting the relevant word. Having found such a topic you may be led by means of hypertext links to other relevant pages.

Alternatively, you may use the instruction manuals supplied with the software. These often contain useful examples for you to follow. You will usually find the item you need by using either the table of contents or the index.

As well as software manuals there are many other instruction manuals available. All technical equipment comes with a manual, from the video and microwave oven to the bicycle.

Find as many manuals as you can and read them. Some will be good and some not so good. The best will give all the detail you need to use the software or equipment and are written without assuming you have any prior knowledge at all. They should not patronise you, but should be written clearly and in layman's terms. Using jargon and not explaining it is a very bad sign in a manual.

IT the Magazine

Magazines and other publications

Magazines and pamphlets are other sources of information. As with other general publications you have to consider the integrity of the information and cross-check with other sources.

Magazines are available for many topics from music through to cars and sports. Whatever information you are seeking may well be available through a magazine.

Activity

List all the magazines you can find that are published for those interested in or working with computers. Do you read any? Which ones and why?

The main advantage of using magazines as information sources is that they are usually up to date, particularly if the subject matter is technical.

The disadvantage is that you may have to read a large number of articles or issues to find the piece for which you are looking. Looking through the table of contents at the beginning of each issue and using the article title or description to tell you the subject with which it deals can reduce this.

Public databases

These are sources of information available to all of us. Some might see the Internet as one, but this is not strictly true, as the data available on the Internet is not stored in the structured method required by a database.

Classifying information

We have looked at various sources of information, all of which we might use. All of these are structured in some way. Either by the record structures of a formal database, the number structures of a spreadsheet or the page structure of an Internet web site.

To structure data into information you need to identify common features. Let us return to the library and look at the catalogue.

We have said it is a record structure. Each book in the library is a record. Each record consists of a number of fields. Each field contains a particular type of information. Let us see if we can classify the individual fields:

- Title
- Author
- Publisher
- ISBN (International Standard Book Number)
- Catalogue number

In this way there are clearly identified areas of data. These classifications will be used when you are searching or sorting the database.

Developing and presenting information

Having identified the data you need it must then be developed to provide you with the required information. There are many processes that you may need to perform upon the identified data to produce appropriately structured information including:

- Search the data
- Sort alphabetically
- Sort numerically
- Produce graphs
- Produce charts
- Calculate values

Artist with easel

There are various different methods of presenting information. Which you use will depend upon the type of information and the circumstances of the presentation. The presentation methods will require that the data be suitably structured to ensure it is easily understood.

We said earlier that most people are familiar with the saying 'A picture is worth a thousand words'. Pictures and illustrations are very important to us. Remember the example we used? A friend is giving you directions to their house. You ask for a map, this makes the journey much simpler – you can see the route you will need to take. The map helps you to understand the information your friend is giving you.

Activity

Pictures and diagrams are essential in industry. How do we build 'flat pack' furniture? Have you ever tried to do this? In what form do the instructions come?

When you are presenting information it is important that you make it attractive and easy to understand. The software applications available today make this very easy with a little practice.

You should investigate the software applications available to you and learn how to use the following:

- Borders
- Charts
- Clip art
- Colour
- Graphics
- Graphs
- Headings
- Highlights
- Shading
- Tables

When you present information remember that you should be making an attractive presentation and not just trying to use all the facilities that the software offers you.

Most numerical information will be easiest to understand when it is presented using graphs or charts. This is simply done in most spreadsheet applications. Start by selecting the figures to be used and following the on-screen instructions for charts.

Databases

Databases are software packages designed to allow different types of data to be stored, retrieved and manipulated. The manipulation may be to provide management reports, operational reports such as lists of customers, etc.

Look at Figure 2.1, the insurance brokers index card (see page 51). Did you realise that a field for the date of birth would be useful? In Figure 2.3 we have included this field. Let us now identify the data types contained in this record.

Surname	Forename(s)		Client number
Jones	Matthew Thomas		99-4625
Address	32 Devises Crescent		
	Anothertown		
	Anyshire		
Postcode	AA2 2P2	**Date of birth**	23-05-73
Telephone	0123-789-9512		

Fig. 2.3 File card with additional data

Each field will contain a particular type of data. These **data types** will include:

● Character
● Date
● Number

It is clear that the date of birth field contains the data type **date**. The name, address and client number fields contain the data type **character**, in some applications this is known as the data type **text**. The client number field is not of the data type **number**, but is a character field. The reason is that the field contents are not used for the purposes of calculation. In Figure 2.4, where we look at the insurance policies held by this client, we see a field **premium**. This field contains data of the

Policy type	Policy number	Expiry	Premium	Client number
				99-4625
Home Contents	13-65654895	06/10/2000	459.76	
Motor	JON654897	02/02/2000	259.91	
Life Assurance	MTJON7955		125.46	
Endowment			759.22	

Fig. 2.4 File card listing insurance held

type number. In this field are contained values that may be totalled or otherwise manipulated to satisfy the needs of the broker.

Activity

In Figure 2.4 what is the key field identifying the motor insurance policy?

Creating a database

We shall now consider an application of the facilities and purposes of the database. We will create a database. For illustration we shall use the Microsoft ® Access package. You may use another application, investigate this to see how you could perform the following.

A racehorse trainer keeps records of the horses in their care, the owners of these horses, and the colours in which they were raced. The colours are the identifying top and cap cover worn by the jockey to enable people to see whose horse is where during the race. Every owner registers his or her colours with the Jockey Club.

So let's look at this trainer's file. We shall call him Peter Winstanley. What information will he need to keep in his file of horses? He will need to identify which horse belongs to which owner as he will need to invoice each owner with their training fee, race entries, vet's bill and shoeing costs. He needs to know what age each horse is as some races are restricted to certain age groups. He also needs to know whether they are male or female for similar reasons.

HorseTbl : Table				
HorseName	**Gender**	**Age**	**Colour**	**OwnerID**
Bobs Your Uncle	C	2	Bright Bay	7
Cheshire Cat	G	5	Bay	6
Chippie	G	8	Chestnut	5
Honeybunch	F	3	Dun	4
Hope and Glory	F	2	Chestnut	1
Jane Doe	M	4	Bay	3
Jilly's Cooper	F	5	Bay	10
Monica	M	7	Bay	10
Not A Hope	G	6	Black	1
Rumplestiltskin	C	2	Grey	2
The Barrel	G	7	Grey	10
Whatsit	G	5	Bay	4
		0		0

Record: 13 of 13

Fig. 2.5 Screen showing data displayed in horse table

He will include the horse's name, its age, sex, and colour (to help with identifying it). As before he will need a key field. The description of a horse will not be only male and female, it will be mare; filly (a young female horse, usually of less than four years); colt (a young male); and gelding (a castrated male horse).

Figure 2.5 shows the data that is held in the horse table. The table does not show all the required data and more data is held in another table. Notice that the owner is represented by a code and not name and address. This is because it is more efficient to store the owner's details in a separate table as this saves repeating the same data.

For example, the owner may own several horses and if each record of a horse included all the relevant owner details it would create a cumbersome file. Therefore, each table has a **relationship** in common. In the tables shown in Figure 2.5 and Figure 2.6 that common item is the owner's code.

As you can see Peter's secretary still has some work to do. The table has its structure determined. There is a field for the each of the following:

- Owner code
- Surname
- Forename
- Address
- Postcode
- Telephone number

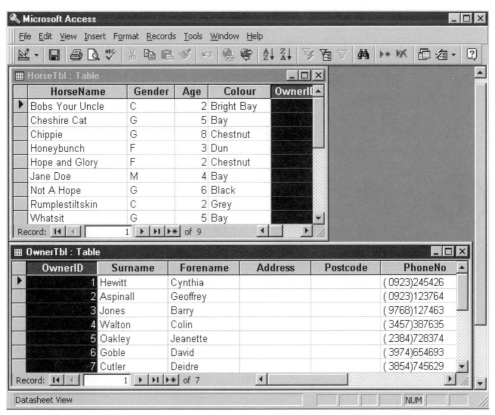

Fig. 2.6 Screen showing the relationship between 'horse table' and 'owner table'

The secretary will need to **amend** the details held on each owner in the table by adding in the addresses and postcodes. This is one of the many editing facilities available in database packages. Should an owner then change their address or other details the records may again be amended.

Activity

Investigate the package you will be using and see what editing facilities are available.

Should Peter take on a new owner and horse then their details will need to be added to the appropriate tables. To **append** details to a table is to add a new row of details.

Activity

What would be the changes to the tables should Peter accept the horse Running Wild, a five-year-old bay gelding owned by John Smithers of 42 Acacia Crescent, Anytown, Anyshire, AA2 3DR whose telephone number is 0159-987-4563?

Let us imagine the owner of Chippie decides to move their horse to another trainer. Then the details of the horse and the related details of its owner will need to be **deleted** from the tables.

Neither of these tables contains details of the colours. These may be held in another table listing the colours as shown in Figure 2.7.

We can clearly see the structure of the database that Peter needs to maintain his data. Some of the tables contain data items that relate to the data held in other tables. For example, every row in the horse table contains the ID number of the relevant owner. This is called a **foreign key**. It is the key field in the owner table and enables the relationship between the two tables to be managed.

Activity

Why is the owner ID in the horse table and the horse names not in the owners table?

Having set up his database Peter Winstanley may need to manipulate the data to produce reports that are useful to him.

For example he may wish to know the names of all the owners of four-year-old horses. He can do this by **querying** the database to show the records of horses whose ages equal four. This is an example of a search using a **relational operator**. The answer to a query using a relational operator can either be **true** or **false**. The age of an animal may either be four, true, or not, false.

There are a range of relational operators available on databases including:

- Equal to (=)
- Less than (<)
- Greater than (>)

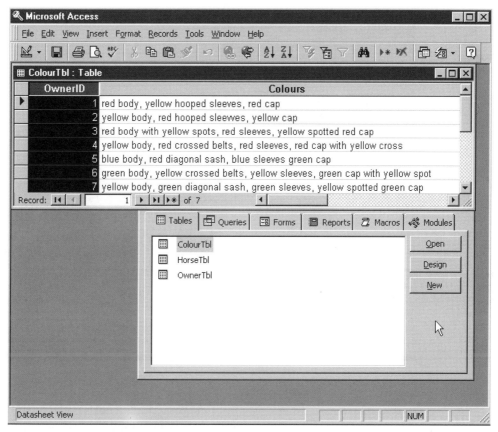

Fig. 2.7 Screen showing table of colours

- Less than or equal to (≤)
- Greater than or equal to (≥)

If we search the database shown for all horses that are four years old the results are as shown in Figure 2.8; as you see only the horse Jane Doe is returned. Alternatively, Peter may need to search his database to discover which horses are older than four **and** geldings. The results of this search are shown in the right-hand corner in Figure 2.8. As can be seen the results are very different, there is no Jane Doe as this horse is not a gelding. This is searching using a **logical operator**.

The following are logical operators:

- AND
- OR
- NOT

In the compilation of reports, data may need to be sorted into some order other than that of the primary key. Perhaps Peter will need a list of owners in alphabetical order. He may then **select** the surname as a **secondary key field** for **sorting**.

As can be seen we have used an index on the owner's table. It is a simple number. Wherever we might need to link data from one table to another then this unique

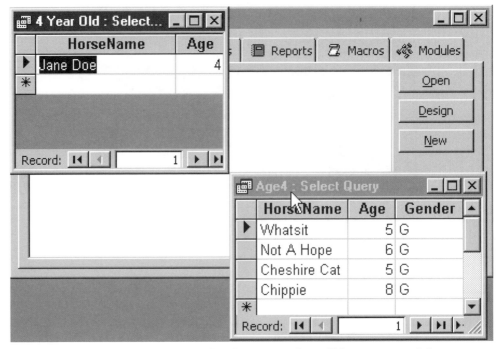

Fig. 2.8 Screen showing result of a query for all horses aged four

identifying field is included. Remember this is called a foreign key. Each horse in the horse table, for example, has a field denoting the owner's code. Each horse also has an index although in the example so far developed it is not used. Its application would probably be in the compilation of invoices to the owners.

There will usually be a user manual for a database. We saw earlier how important instruction manuals can be. Remember that the user will need instructions presented as easily understood steps to enable them to achieve the results they need. These instructions should be written in plain English and without any unnecessary jargon. However, in some circumstances jargon can prevent a manual from becoming very wordy, if this is the case then the jargon should be simply explained and then used.

Activity

Create this database yourself and use it to practise all these activities:

- Entering data (add more horses and owners)
- Editing data that is entered to the tables (suppose one of the owners has moved address)
- Sorting the data into a different order
- Searching the records, perhaps for all geldings aged four or over
- Querying the database to find the names of all horses that are geldings and over the age of four, and show the owners colours
- Writing a set of instructions for Peter and his secretary to enable them to use the database

Spreadsheets

Earlier in this section we looked at how pictures can be used to help people understand information. Sometimes, however, a picture may not be enough. Suppose a firm of architects is designing a new sports complex that will consist of several interlinked buildings. While plans and diagrams can be used to show what the complex will look like, most people will find a three-dimensional **model** more helpful. In the same way, car designers begin by drawing pictures and plans of new car designs and then create models to show what the new car will look like 'in the round'.

This type of model is called a **physical model**. It is something that you can see, handle and measure. This type of model is a representation of something that exists, or will exist, in the real world. Many children's toys are models of real things. By playing with toys such as dolls and model cars, children begin to learn about the real world.

Models are used a great deal in the business world. A manufacturing company will need to predict its likely profits over periods of time. Calculations will be performed which take into account the costs of manufacturing the company's goods and the income that will be generated from the sale of these goods. The effects of factors such as increases in the costs of raw materials and wages can be predicted. These calculations are also a model. They are not physical models, but mathematical representations of situations. Such models are known as **logical models**.

These models are based on mathematical calculations and so follow clearly defined rules. The profit calculation can be written down as:

Profit = (Income from sales) – (Cost of manufacture)

This equation is the **rule** that is used in this very simple model. The values for income and costs, figures that can be changed as required, are the **input variables** of the model. Using this model, it is possible to **predict** what would happen to the profits if the company sold its goods at a higher price or if the manufacturing costs increased. These predictions are made by changing the figures for income or costs and seeing what effect these changes have on the profit figure. The profit figure is the **information output** from the model.

Situations which can be defined mathematically in this way are very suitable for **computer modelling** using **spreadsheet** applications software. Spreadsheets allow the user to enter numerical data and manipulate it in various ways. There are many applications of spreadsheet models. Some examples include financial forecasting and budgeting, journey planning, modelling queues of people at supermarket checkouts, modelling traffic flow on roads and animal population forecasting. In building one of these models, the user will have to decide on the rules and the input variables which are required. You will set up some computer models yourself as part of your course.

In these examples, the models are software representations of real situations and can be used to predict the effects of changes. A model allows the user to ask **what if** questions such as: 'What would be the effect on journey times if the new bypass opens?' or 'What would happen to the length of the queues at the checkouts if we opened another checkout?'

Another application of modelling with which you may well be very familiar is computer **games**. A computer game uses software to model a situation for entertainment purposes. Some of these games are computer versions of existing activities. For example, the Solitaire game that comes with Microsoft Windows ® is a computerised version of the card game you probably know as Patience. There are also games which mimic sports such as snooker and football. Other games are based around activities such as driving a car or flying an aeroplane. These games model, with varying degrees of realism, actual situations. Other games, such as treasure hunts, are based entirely on fantasy.

Computer games are based on rules, just like the mathematical models. However, the rules used in computer games tend to be very complex and most of them are hidden from the player. A treasure hunt wouldn't be much fun if you knew exactly how it worked – there would be no element of challenge or the unexpected. In some games, there are rules that the player can change. If you are playing the Solitaire game, for instance, you can alter things like the number of cards you turn over at a time and the method of scoring which is used. What you can't change is the way in which the pack of cards is shuffled. The input variables to games are the players' responses to the situations which are presented to them.

Activity

With which computer games are you familiar? Can you suggest what sort of rules these games use? Can you change any of the rules? What are the input variables to the games?

Computer models can be used for **training**. One such example is the use of **flight simulators** to train pilots. Using a flight simulator, a trainee pilot can experience what it is like to fly an aircraft without the expense or risks of the actual situation. They can receive basic training before flying a real aircraft. Flight simulators can also be used to teach pilots about the landing routes and conditions at new airports. They can also be used to allow pilots to experience safely emergencies such as an aircraft fire or an engine failure.

Another training application of computer models is **business games**. In these, students are presented with a business scenario and then must make decisions about running the business, such as which products to make and what prices to charge. As the students enter their decisions, the system responds with further information until the students are successful or the business fails.

In **weather forecasting**, computer models are used to predict weather patterns. These models take data from a variety of sources such as satellites and weather stations and compare it with previously collected and analysed data in order to predict the future pattern.

Whenever you use a model, be it a mathematical model or a game, it is very important to always be aware that the model is only a **representation** of the real world. The real world is very complex and in order to produce models it is necessary to make **assumptions**. In order to create the model, simplifications will be necessary. The better the rules used, the more closely the model will mimic the reality, but it is still only a model and the outputs should be used with this fact in mind.

Spreadsheet basics

As we said earlier spreadsheets are applications packages which are used to process numerical data. Remember, they are used in business, science, engineering, and geography.

Earlier we described a spreadsheet as an electronic sheet of paper on which you can carry out calculations. Suppose that you are the Sales Manager for a small company. This company divides its sales area into three regions and each month you need to calculate the total sales for the company. You also need to keep totals for each of the individual regions. How would you do this manually?

You would probably set up a table similar to the one in Table 2.4. Each month you would enter the sales figures in the appropriate places. To calculate the total sales for a month you would add up the figures across the row for that month. To calculate the total sales for a particular region, you would total the figures in the appropriate column.

Table 2.4 2000 monthly sales figures

2000 MONTHLY SALES FIGURES (£)	Region 1	Region 2	Region 3	Totals	
January	1,000.00	1,203.00	1,699.00	£3,902.00	
February	768.00	567.00	457.00	£1,792.00	
March	646.00	234.00	678.00	£1,558.00	
April	1,289.00	780.00	987.00	£3,056.00	
May	590.00	450.00	1,200.00	£2,240.00	
June	2,009.00	300.00	300.00	£2,609.00	—June total
July	743.00	653.00	789.00	£2,185.00	
August	859.00	790.00	456.00	£2,105.00	
September	1,002.00	1,473.00	976.00	£3,451.00	
October	880.00	876.00	340.00	£2,096.00	
November	1,356.00	1,287.00	1,598.00	£4,241.00	
December	2,003.00	3,006.00	3,100.00	£8,109.00	
Totals	£13,145.00	£11,619.00	£12,580.00	£37,344.00	

Region 2 total

A spreadsheet package will allow you to carry out exactly the same calculations, except that it will do them faster and if you need to make any changes to the figures, the totals can be easily recalculated.

In the next section, we will look at some of the facilities you will find in a typical spreadsheet package. The details will vary from package to package, so you should consult the user manuals and the on-line help for the particular package you have access to for more detailed information.

Spreadsheet layout

We have said that the basic layout of a spreadsheet is a table with vertical **columns** and horizontal **rows**. The columns are labelled with letters across the top of the table and the rows with numbers down the left-hand side.

Activity

What is the cell reference of the cell identified in Figure 2.2 (see page 59)?
   How many rows are there in a Microsoft ® Excel worksheet?
   How many columns?

Spreadsheet data

You enter data onto a spreadsheet by selecting the required cell and typing in the data. Cells can contain three different types of data:

- Text
- Data
- Formulae

Characters can be typed into cells. You will probably use text mainly for spreadsheet titles and row and column headings. These are known as **labels**. Text in spreadsheets can be formatted using a range of font styles and sizes and attributes such as bold and italic. Different colours can also be used. Text can be aligned within a cell – centre, left and right alignment is possible.

   Numbers in spreadsheets can be formatted in a variety of ways. They can be **integers**, i.e. whole numbers such as 3, 14, 89 or **real numbers** with decimal places such as 23.00 or 2.123. Numbers can be formatted as **currency**. In this case, currency symbols such as £ or $ are added automatically to the numbers. Numbers can also be formatted as **percentages**, **fractions** or in **scientific** format. Numbers can be formatted with different fonts, colours and alignments in a similar way to text.

   Dates can be entered into cells using several formats such as 10/10/00 or 10-Oct-2000. Fonts, colours and alignment can be selected as before.

   Formulae are a very important part of a spreadsheet. Formulae allow the contents of a cell to be calculated from information stored in other parts of the spreadsheet. Formulae are used for arithmetic, for example to add up the contents of a column of cells. Formulae can also contain functions to calculate values such as averages or square roots or to generate random numbers. Formulae can also be used to compare values using operators such as =, < and >. You will see how different types of formulae are used below.

Setting up a spreadsheet

Let's go back to your problem as Sales Manager.

Activity

How would you set up a spreadsheet to calculate the sales figures?

	A	B	C	D	E	F
1	2000 Monthly Sales Figures					
2						
3		Region 1	Region 2	Region 3	Total sales	
4	Jan	£1,000.00	£1,203.00	£1,699.00		
5	Feb	£768.00	£567.00	£457.00		
6	Mar	£646.00	£234.00	£678.00		
7	Apr	£1,289.00	£780.00	£987.00		
8	May	£590.00	£450.00	£1,200.00		
9	Jun	£2,009.00	£300.00	£300.00		
10	Jul	£743.00	£653.00	£789.00		
11	Aug	£859.00	£790.00	£456.00		
12	Sept	£1,002.00	£1,473.00	£976.00		
13	Oct	£880.00	£876.00	£340.00		
14	Nov	£1,356.00	£1,287.00	£1,598.00		
15	Dec	£2,003.00	£3,006.00	£3,100.00		
16	Totals					
17						

Fig. 2.9 A sales figures spreadsheet

Figure 2.9 shows how a spreadsheet could be set up and the data entered. The main title, column and row headings and the sales figures have been entered. The headings have been formatted with bold text. The sales figures have been formatted as currency. Note the alignment of the data in the cells. The **column width** of column A has also been reduced to improve the appearance of the spreadsheet.

Next, we need formulae to calculate the row and column totals. Figure 2.10 shows two ways this could be done. The formula in cell E4 was entered by typing in the actual cell references of the cells in the row which need to be totalled. This is perfectly acceptable, but, if there are a lot of cell references to enter, this could be rather tedious. The formula in cell E5 shows a different way of entering a formula to produce the same total. In this case, the **SUM** function has been used and the required cells selected.

Once the first formula to total a row has been entered, it can then be **copied** to the other cells in the total sales column – you do not need to type the formula into each cell. Figure 2.11 shows the spreadsheet with all the formulae in place. When you copy a formula, the cell references are automatically changed to the appropriate references. Later, we will look at examples where you will need to prevent this happening. Figure 2.12 shows the completed spreadsheet, with the results of the calculations.

Once the spreadsheet is set up, it is very easy to make changes. Suppose that you need to update the November figure for Region 2. All you need to do is type the new figure into cell C14, and the November row total and the Region 2 column total will be automatically recalculated. This is shown in Figure 2.13.

	A	B	C	D	E
1	2000 Monthly Sales Figures				
2					
3		Region 1	Region 2	Region 3	Total sales
4	Jan	1000	1203	1699	=B4+C4+D4
5	Feb	768	567	457	=SUM(B5:D5)
6	Mar	646	234	678	
7	Apr	1289	780	987	
8	May	590	450	1200	
9	Jun	2009	300	300	
10	Jul	743	653	789	
11	Aug	859	790	456	
12	Sept	1002	1473	976	
13	Oct	880	876	340	
14	Nov	1356	1287	1598	
15	Dec	2003	3006	3100	
16	Totals				
17					

Fig. 2.10 The sales figures spreadsheet showing formulae that could be used

	A	B	C	D	E	F
1	2000 Monthly Sales Figures					
2						
3		Region 1	Region 2	Region 3	Total sales	
4	Jan	1000	1203	1699	=SUM(B4:D4)	
5	Feb	768	567	457	=SUM(B5:D5)	
6	Mar	646	234	678	=SUM(B6:D6)	
7	Apr	1289	780	987	=SUM(B7:D7)	
8	May	590	450	1200	=SUM(B8:D8)	
9	Jun	2009	300	300	=SUM(B9:D9)	
10	Jul	743	653	789	=SUM(B10:D10)	
11	Aug	859	790	456	=SUM(B11:D11)	
12	Sept	1002	1473	976	=SUM(B12:D12)	
13	Oct	880	876	340	=SUM(B13:D13)	
14	Nov	1356	1287	1598	=SUM(B14:D14)	
15	Dec	2003	3006	3100	=SUM(B15:D15)	
16	Totals	=SUM(B4:B15)	=SUM(C4:C15)	=SUM(D4:D15)	=SUM(E4:E15)	
17						

Fig. 2.11 The completed spreadsheet showing all the formulae in place

	A	B	C	D	E	F
1	2000 Monthly Sales Figures					
2						
3		Region 1	Region 2	Region 3	Total sales	
4	Jan	£1,000.00	£1,203.00	£1,699.00	£3,902.00	
5	Feb	£768.00	£567.00	£457.00	£1,792.00	
6	Mar	£646.00	£234.00	£678.00	£1,558.00	
7	Apr	£1,289.00	£780.00	£987.00	£3,056.00	
8	May	£590.00	£450.00	£1,200.00	£2,240.00	
9	Jun	£2,009.00	£300.00	£300.00	£2,609.00	
10	Jul	£743.00	£653.00	£789.00	£2,185.00	
11	Aug	£859.00	£790.00	£456.00	£2,105.00	
12	Sept	£1,002.00	£1,473.00	£976.00	£3,451.00	
13	Oct	£880.00	£876.00	£340.00	£2,096.00	
14	Nov	£1,356.00	£1,287.00	£1,598.00	£4,241.00	
15	Dec	£2,003.00	£3,006.00	£3,100.00	£8,109.00	
16	Totals	£13,145.00	£11,619.00	£12,580.00	£37,344.00	
17						

Fig. 2.12 The completed spreadsheet showing calculated values

	A	B	C	D	E	F	G
1	2000 Monthly Sales Figures						
2							
3		Region 1	Region 2	Region 3	Total sales		
4	Jan	£1,000.00	£1,203.00	£1,699.00	£3,902.00		
5	Feb	£768.00	£567.00	£457.00	£1,792.00		
6	Mar	£646.00	£234.00	£678.00	£1,558.00		
7	Apr	£1,289.00	£780.00	£987.00	£3,056.00		
8	May	£590.00	£450.00	£1,200.00	£2,240.00		
9	Jun	£2,009.00	£300.00	£300.00	£2,609.00		
10	Jul	£743.00	£653.00	£789.00	£2,185.00		
11	Aug	£859.00	£790.00	£456.00	£2,105.00		
12	Sept	£1,002.00	£1,473.00	£976.00	£3,451.00		
13	Oct	£880.00	£876.00	£340.00	£2,096.00		
14	Nov	£1,356.00	£2,000.00	£1,598.00	£4,954.00		
15	Dec	£2,003.00	£3,006.00	£3,100.00	£8,109.00		
16	Totals	£13,145.00	£12,332.00	£12,580.00	£38,057.00		
17	*new value*						
18						*recalculations*	

Fig. 2.13 The completed spreadsheet showing new value and recalculations

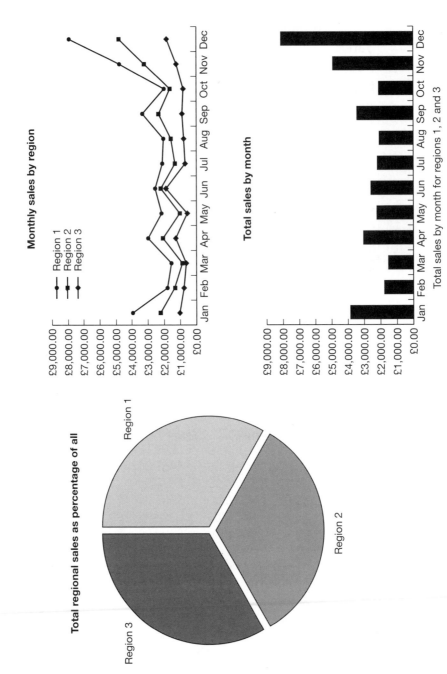

Fig. 2.14 Sample charts from the spreadsheet

Other spreadsheet features

Data in the cells of a spreadsheet can be **copied** and **moved** to other cells if required. As has already been mentioned, cell references in formulae are automatically updated unless you take steps to prevent this.

Extra columns and rows can be **inserted** into a spreadsheet if required or they can be **deleted** if necessary.

The data in a spreadsheet can be displayed in **graph** form. A range of chart formats is available, including area, bar, line and pie charts and 3D versions of these forms. Figure 2.14, shows some of these chart types, using the data from the sales figures spreadsheet.

Spreadsheets are widely used as flat file databases. That is, all the data is stored in one table, unlike the relational databases we were looking at earlier. A teacher may set up a spreadsheet to maintain the records of student marks during a course, as shown in Figure 2.15. As the marks are input to the spreadsheet an IF function awards the grades according to the criteria. The criteria might be that if a mark greater than 85 is earned then a grade A is awarded. If the mark is less than 85 but greater than 65 then a grade B is awarded. For a mark between 65 and 50 a grade C is awarded, between 35 and 50 a grade E, less than 35 is an F grade. The whole formula is:

=IF(C3>85,"A",IF(C3>65,"B",IF(C3>50,"C",IF(C3>40,"D",IF(C3>35,"E","F")))))

Here we see that if the contents of the cell C3 are greater than 85 then an A grade is awarded. If that is not the case then the spreadsheet looks to see if another condition is true, if C3 is greater than 65 then a 'B' grade is awarded, etc.

Let us add another column that gives an average grade from the figures given and let us suppose that the teacher wants to see all those students whose average grade is C or above. Modern spreadsheet packages will enable you to filter data held. The bottom part of Figure 2.15 shows how this looks.

Activity

Try this as an exercise for yourself. What formula do you need to give the average grade awarded? What other function can you use to achieve this?

Spreadsheet packages offer a range of **printing** facilities. You can choose to print a spreadsheet in portrait or landscape orientation and you can set the page margins. You may be able to centre the spreadsheet on the page or adjust the size of the spreadsheet to fit the page.

As with all applications, you will need to **save** and **back up** your spreadsheets regularly.

Activity

Explore the range of facilities that are available in the spreadsheet package you use. Set up some spreadsheets for yourself. Save and print your work.

	A	B	C	D	E	F	G
1			assignment 1		assignment 2		
2	▼	▼	marks awarded (/100) ▼	grade awarded ▼	marks awarded (/100) ▼	grade awarded ▼	Average grade awarded ▼
3	Bertrand	Roger	51	C	55	C	C
4	Brittain	Helouise	72	B	81	B	B
5	Georgiou	John	91	A	89	A	A
6	Gresholm	David	31	F	33	F	F
7	Harriott	Karen	56	C	49	D	C
8	Ho	Jean	56	C	62	C	C
9	Jones	George	43	D	53	C	D
10	Loughlin	Anne	29	F	13	F	F
11	Loughlin	Maggie	39	E	43	D	D
12	Patel	Najeek	58	C	53	C	C
13	Patten	Susan	62	C	67	B	C
14	Smithers	Angela	23	F	39	E	F
15	Wiltshaw	William	43	D	46	D	D
16							

	A	B	C	D	E	F	G
1			assignment 1		assignment 2		
2	▼	▼	marks awarded (/100) ▼	grade awarded ▼	marks awarded (/100) ▼	grade awarded ▼	Average grade awarded ▼
3	Bertrand	Roger	51	C	55	C	C
4	Brittain	Helouise	72	B	81	B	B
5	Georgiou	John	91	A	89	A	A
7	Harriott	Karen	56	C	49	D	C
8	Ho	Jean	56	C	62	C	C
12	Patel	Najeek	58	C	53	C	C
13	Patten	Susan	62	C	67	B	C
16							

Fig. 2.15 Student marks before and after applying the data filter

Modelling with spreadsheets

There are several stages to building a spreadsheet model. First of all, you will need to identify the data required – the **input variables.** Then, you must define the **rules** of the model – the calculations that will be necessary.

The spreadsheet **layout** must be designed. This stage is often best done on paper, so that you can produce a layout which is easy to understand. You will need to decide on column headings, cell formats, etc. You will need to work out the formulae required.

Next, you will set up the spreadsheet and enter the data and formulae into the appropriate places. You can then begin to use the model, changing variables and looking at the results. You may wish to produce graphs of the results. You will print out the results.

You will, of course, save your model at regular intervals and keep backup copies!

These stages will be illustrated with several examples. These examples have been created using the Microsoft ® Excel package.

A financial model – a break-even model

Earlier, a very simple equation was used to show that the profit a business makes depends on its income from sales and the production costs incurred:

Profit = (Income from sales) – (Cost of manufacture)

Obviously, in order to make a profit, the income from sales must exceed manufacturing costs. There is a point at which the income and costs match – this is the **break-even point**.

The following example shows how a break-even model can be set up.

Consider the case of a small company that makes soft toys. The company is thinking of making and selling a new design of teddy bear and needs to know how profitable this venture is likely to be. In particular, they need to know how many bears they will need to sell every month in order to make a profit.

The costs incurred in making the teddy bears fall into two categories: variable costs and fixed costs.

The **variable costs** depend on the number of bears made and, in this case, are the costs of the materials, the fur, stuffing, etc., needed to make each bear. The company has calculated that the materials for each bear will cost them £3.25.

Each month, the company has to meet expenses such as the rent of its premises. These expenses do not depend on the number of bears made and sold – they are **fixed costs**. The company's fixed costs are £800 per month.

The company is planning to sell the teddy bears at a price of £8.50 each.

A spreadsheet model can be used to show how many bears must be sold to balance the income from sales with the costs of making the bears.

The rules for the model can be written down like this:

Income from sales = Selling price per bear × Number of bears sold

Manufacturing cost = Fixed cost + (Material cost × Number of bears sold)

Figure 2.16 shows a spreadsheet set up to find the break-even point. The formulae used are shown in Figure 2.17.

The fixed cost, variable cost per bear and the selling price are entered into cells at the top of the spreadsheet. The number of bears sold is entered in column A and the fixed monthly cost in column B.

	A	B	C	D	E	F
1	BREAK-EVEN MODEL - TEDDY BEARS					
2						
3	Monthly fixed cost		£800.00			
4	Variable cost per bear		£3.25			
5	Selling price per bear		£8.50			
6						
7						
8	Quantity sold	Fixed cost	Variable cost	Total cost	Income from sales	
9	25	£800.00	£81.25	£881.25	£212.50	
10	50	£800.00	£162.50	£962.50	£425.00	
11	75	£800.00	£243.75	£1,043.75	£637.50	
12	100	£800.00	£325.00	£1,125.00	£850.00	
13	125	£800.00	£406.25	£1,206.25	£1,062.50	
14	150	£800.00	£487.50	£1,287.50	£1,275.00	
15	175	£800.00	£568.75	£1,368.75	£1,487.50	
16	200	£800.00	£650.00	£1,450.00	£1,700.00	
17	225	£800.00	£731.25	£1,531.25	£1,912.50	
18	250	£800.00	£812.50	£1,612.50	£2,125.00	
19	275	£800.00	£893.75	£1,693.75	£2,337.50	
20	300	£800.00	£975.00	£1,775.00	£2,550.00	
21						

Fig. 2.16 A break-even model

The formula in column C calculates the variable cost of making the appropriate number of bears by multiplying the number from column A by the variable cost per bear that has been entered in cell C4. Note the use of the $ signs in this formula. We said earlier that when you copy a formula, the cell references are automatically updated unless you prevent this happening. In the case of this formula, we want the reference to the cell in column A to be updated as the formula is copied down column C, but not the reference to cell C4, as this must stay the same. The $ signs 'lock' the cell reference and prevent it from being updated. A cell reference locked in this way is known as an **absolute cell reference.**

The formula in column D calculates the total cost by adding the fixed and variable costs and the formula in column E calculates the income obtained by selling the appropriate number of bears. Note the use of absolute cell references again.

	A	B	C	D	E	
1	BREAK-EVEN MODEL - TEDDY BEARS					
2						
3	Monthly fixed cost		800			
4	Variable cost per bear		3.25			
5	Selling price per bear		8.5			
6						
7						
8	Quantity sold	Fixed cost	Variable cost	Total cost	Income from sales	
9	25	=$C$3	=$C$4*A9	=B9+C9	=$C$5*A9	
10	50	=$C$3	=$C$4*A10	=B10+C10	=$C$5*A10	
11	75	=$C$3	=$C$4*A11	=B11+C11	=$C$5*A11	
12	100	=$C$3	=$C$4*A12	=B12+C12	=$C$5*A12	
13	125	=$C$3	=$C$4*A13	=B13+C13	=$C$5*A13	
14	150	=$C$3	=$C$4*A14	=B14+C14	=$C$5*A14	
15	175	=$C$3	=$C$4*A15	=B15+C15	=$C$5*A15	
16	200	=$C$3	=$C$4*A16	=B16+C16	=$C$5*A16	
17	225	=$C$3	=$C$4*A17	=B17+C17	=$C$5*A17	
18	250	=$C$3	=$C$4*A18	=B18+C18	=$C$5*A18	
19	275	=$C$3	=$C$4*A19	=B19+C19	=$C$5*A19	
20	300	=$C$3	=$C$4*A20	=B20+C20	=$C$5*A20	
21						

Fig. 2.17 The formulae used in the break-even model

If you look at Figure 2.16, you will see that the break-even point comes between 150 and 175 bears sold. At 150 bears, the income is slightly less than the cost of manufacture. By the time 175 bears have been sold, the company is making a profit.

To find the exact break-even point, two more versions of the spreadsheet are used.

In Figure 2.18, the quantity sold ranges from 150 to 175 in steps of five. The break-even point is between 150 and 155 bears, so a final version of the spreadsheet, covering this range in single steps is produced, showing that the company makes a profit with the 153rd bear sold. This is shown in Figure 2.19.

It is sometimes helpful to show the break-even point graphically, as in Figure 2.20.

Once the model has been set up, it can be used to test the effects on the company's profits of changes in the fixed or variable costs or increasing or reducing the selling price of the bears. That's why these figures are entered into cells at the top of the spreadsheet, rather than directly into the formulae themselves. If the company wants to check the effect of increasing the price of the bears, only the figure in cell C5 needs to be altered and this change will automatically be reflected in all the formulae containing the C5 cell reference.

	A	B	C	D	E
1	BREAK-EVEN MODEL - TEDDY BEARS				
2					
3	Monthly fixed cost		£800.00		
4	Variable cost per bear		£3.25		
5	Selling price per bear		£8.50		
6					
7					
8	Quantity sold	Fixed cost	Variable cost	Total cost	Income from sales
9	150	800.00	487.50	1287.50	1275.00
10	155	800.00	503.75	1303.75	1317.50
11	160	800.00	520.00	1320.00	1360.00
12	165	800.00	536.25	1336.25	1402.50
13	170	800.00	552.50	1352.50	1445.00
14	175	800.00	568.75	1368.75	1487.50
15					

Fig. 2.18 The second version of the break-even model

	A	B	C	D	E	F
1	BREAK-EVEN MODEL - TEDDY BEARS					
2						
3	Monthly fixed cost		£800.00			
4	Variable cost per bear		£3.25			
5	Selling price per bear		£8.50			
6						
7						
8	Quantity sold	Fixed cost	Variable cost	Total cost	Income from sales	
9	150	800.00	487.50	1287.50	1275.00	
10	151	800.00	490.75	1290.75	1283.50	
11	152	800.00	494.00	1294.00	1292.00	
12	153	800.00	497.25	1297.25	1300.50	
13	154	800.00	500.50	1300.50	1309.00	
14	155	800.00	503.75	1303.75	1317.50	
15	156	800.00	507.00	1307.00	1326.00	
16						

Fig. 2.19 The final version of the break-even model

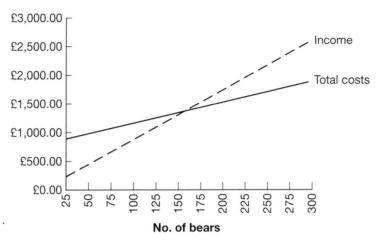

Break-even chart

Fig. 2.20 The break-even graph

A scientific model – a chemical reaction

Using a spreadsheet is one way in which IT can be used to create a model. Such a model can be used to predict the pattern of a chemical reaction. Figure 2.21 shows how this can be done.

Compound A reacts with Compound B to produce Compound C. The rate of the reaction is given by the mathematical equation:

Rate of formation of C = k × [Concentration of A] × [Concentration of B]

where k is a constant that is measured experimentally.

The spreadsheet uses the equation to calculate the rate at which Compound C will be formed. The formulae used are shown in Figure 2.22.

This type of model is used extensively in the chemical industry. A chemical engineer would set up a model like this to predict the course of a reaction on a chemical plant so as to be able to optimise the production of required chemicals. Similar models can be used to predict the effects of changes in temperature of reaction mixtures. This information can be used to determine safe operating limits for reactions.

Activity

Try creating this spreadsheet and make a chart of the three columns headed Conc. of A, Conc. of B and Conc. of C. Use a line chart.

Using functions in a model – tossing a coin

Both the models examined so far have been based on arithmetical calculations. Spreadsheet formulae can also contain special functions. One such function can be used to generate random numbers. This function can be used in a spreadsheet model that simulates the tossing of a coin.

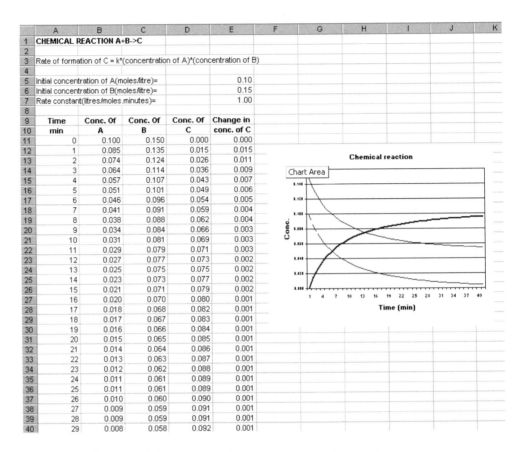

	A	B	C	D	E
1	CHEMICAL REACTION A+B->C				
3	Rate of formation of C = k*(concentration of A)*(concentration of B)				
5	Initial concentration of A(moles/litre)=			0.10	
6	Initial concentration of B(moles/litre)=			0.15	
7	Rate constant(litres/moles.minutes)=			1.00	
9	Time	Conc. Of	Conc. Of	Conc. Of	Change in
10	min	A	B	C	conc. of C
11	0	0.100	0.150	0.000	0.000
12	1	0.085	0.135	0.015	0.015
13	2	0.074	0.124	0.026	0.011
14	3	0.064	0.114	0.036	0.009
15	4	0.057	0.107	0.043	0.007
16	5	0.051	0.101	0.049	0.006
17	6	0.046	0.096	0.054	0.005
18	7	0.041	0.091	0.059	0.004
19	8	0.038	0.088	0.062	0.004
20	9	0.034	0.084	0.066	0.003
21	10	0.031	0.081	0.069	0.003
22	11	0.029	0.079	0.071	0.003
23	12	0.027	0.077	0.073	0.002
24	13	0.025	0.075	0.075	0.002
25	14	0.023	0.073	0.077	0.002
26	15	0.021	0.071	0.079	0.002
27	16	0.020	0.070	0.080	0.001
28	17	0.018	0.068	0.082	0.001
29	18	0.017	0.067	0.083	0.001
30	19	0.016	0.066	0.084	0.001
31	20	0.015	0.065	0.085	0.001
32	21	0.014	0.064	0.086	0.001
33	22	0.013	0.063	0.087	0.001
34	23	0.012	0.062	0.088	0.001
35	24	0.011	0.061	0.089	0.001
36	25	0.011	0.061	0.089	0.001
37	26	0.010	0.060	0.090	0.001
38	27	0.009	0.059	0.091	0.001
39	28	0.009	0.059	0.091	0.001
40	29	0.008	0.058	0.092	0.001

Fig. 2.21 A spreadsheet modelling a chemical reaction

When you toss a coin, there is a one in two chance of the result being heads. If you generate a random number between zero and one, there is a similar chance of the number being less than 0.5 ($\frac{1}{2}$). Therefore, you can use the random number function to simulate the tossing of a coin.

Figure 2.23 shows a spreadsheet model that calculates the number of heads resulting from 20 coin tosses. The formulae used are shown in Figure 2.24.

Let's look at how the formulae work.

The chance of a head result is 0.5, so this value is entered into cell H5 (see Figure 2.23).

The formula in column D contains the function that generates a random number between zero and one.

The formulae in columns B and C make use of the IF logical function. This function carries out a test on the value in a cell. The format is:

= IF(logical_test, value_if_true, value_if_false)

This means that if the result of the test is TRUE, the function returns one result. If the result of the test is FALSE, a different result is returned.

The formula in column B compares the random number which has been generated in column B with the value in cell H5. If the random number is greater than 0.5,

	A	B	C	D	E
1	CHEMICAL REACTION A+B->C				
2					
3	Rate of formation of C = k*(concentration of A)*(concentration of B)				
4					
5	Initial concentration of A(moles/litre)=				0.1
6	Initial concentration of B(moles/litre)=				0.15
7	Rate constant(litres/moles.minutes)=				1
8					
9	Time	Conc. Of	Conc. Of	Conc. Of	Change in
10	min	A	B	C	conc. of C
11	0	=E5	=E6	0	0
12	=A11+1	=B11-E12	=C11-E12	=D11+E12	=(B11*C11*$E$7)
13	=A12+1	=B12-E13	=C12-E13	=D12+E13	=(B12*C12*$E$7)
14	=A13+1	=B13-E14	=C13-E14	=D13+E14	=(B13*C13*$E$7)
15	=A14+1	=B14-E15	=C14-E15	=D14+E15	=(B14*C14*$E$7)
16	=A15+1	=B15-E16	=C15-E16	=D15+E16	=(B15*C15*$E$7)
17	=A16+1	=B16-E17	=C16-E17	=D16+E17	=(B16*C16*$E$7)
18	=A17+1	=B17-E18	=C17-E18	=D17+E18	=(B17*C17*$E$7)
19	=A18+1	=B18-E19	=C18-E19	=D18+E19	=(B18*C18*$E$7)
20	=A19+1	=B19-E20	=C19-E20	=D19+E20	=(B19*C19*$E$7)
21	=A20+1	=B20-E21	=C20-E21	=D20+E21	=(B20*C20*$E$7)
22	=A21+1	=B21-E22	=C21-E22	=D21+E22	=(B21*C21*$E$7)
23	=A22+1	=B22-E23	=C22-E23	=D22+E23	=(B22*C22*$E$7)
24	=A23+1	=B23-E24	=C23-E24	=D23+E24	=(B23*C23*$E$7)
25	=A24+1	=B24-E25	=C24-E25	=D24+E25	=(B24*C24*$E$7)
26	=A25+1	=B25-E26	=C25-E26	=D25+E26	=(B25*C25*$E$7)
27	=A26+1	=B26-E27	=C26-E27	=D26+E27	=(B26*C26*$E$7)
28	=A27+1	=B27-E28	=C27-E28	=D27+E28	=(B27*C27*$E$7)
29	=A28+1	=B28-E29	=C28-E29	=D28+E29	=(B28*C28*$E$7)
30	=A29+1	=B29-E30	=C29-E30	=D29+E30	=(B29*C29*$E$7)
31	=A30+1	=B30-E31	=C30-E31	=D30+E31	=(B30*C30*$E$7)
32	=A31+1	=B31-E32	=C31-E32	=D31+E32	=(B31*C31*$E$7)
33	=A32+1	=B32-E33	=C32-E33	=D32+E33	=(B32*C32*$E$7)
34	=A33+1	=B33-E34	=C33-E34	=D33+E34	=(B33*C33*$E$7)
35	=A34+1	=B34-E35	=C34-E35	=D34+E35	=(B34*C34*$E$7)
36	=A35+1	=B35-E36	=C35-E36	=D35+E36	=(B35*C35*$E$7)
37	=A36+1	=B36-E37	=C36-E37	=D36+E37	=(B36*C36*$E$7)
38	=A37+1	=B37-E38	=C37-E38	=D37+E38	=(B37*C37*$E$7)
39	=A38+1	=B38-E39	=C38-E39	=D38+E39	=(B38*C38*$E$7)
40	=A39+1	=B39-E40	=C39-E40	=D39+E40	=(B39*C39*$E$7)

Fig. 2.22 The formulae used in the chemical reaction model

the test is TRUE and the formula gives the result "TAILS" and displays this in the cell. If the random number is less than 0.5, the test result is FALSE and the result "HEADS" is returned. Notice the use of the absolute cell reference.

The formula in column C also uses an IF function and looks at the result produced by the formula in column B. If the result displayed in the cell in column B is "HEADS", then the column C formula gives a result of '1'. If the result in column B is not "HEADS", then the result '0' is given. The formula in Column C also totals the number of "HEAD" results.

	A	B	C	D	E	F	G	H
1	TOSSING A COIN							
2								
3								
4	Throw	Result	Tot.heads					
5	1	HEADS	1	0.076756		Chance of "heads"		0.5
6	2	TAILS	1	0.632407				
7	3	HEADS	2	0.076003				
8	4	HEADS	3	0.036392				
9	5	TAILS	3	0.620491				
10	6	HEADS	4	0.049625				
11	7	TAILS	4	0.581665				
12	8	TAILS	4	0.745736				
13	9	HEADS	5	0.085621				
14	10	HEADS	6	0.095048				
15	11	TAILS	6	0.677355				
16	12	TAILS	6	0.516102				
17	13	TAILS	6	0.849749				
18	14	TAILS	6	0.597463				
19	15	TAILS	6	0.893309				
20	16	HEADS	7	0.398138				
21	17	HEADS	8	0.326465				
22	18	HEADS	9	0.426219				
23	19	HEADS	10	0.104779				
24	20	HEADS	11	0.245401				
25								

Fig. 2.23 A spreadsheet to model tossing a coin

	A	B	C	D	E	F	G
2							
3							
4	Throw	Result	Tot.heads				
5	1	=IF(D5>$H$5,"TAILS","HEADS")	=IF(B5="HEADS",1,0)	=RAND()		Chance of "heads"	0.5
6	2	=IF(D6>$H$5,"TAILS","HEADS")	=IF(B6="HEADS",1,0)+C5	=RAND()			
7	3	=IF(D7>$H$5,"TAILS","HEADS")	=IF(B7="HEADS",1,0)+C6	=RAND()			
8	4	=IF(D8>$H$5,"TAILS","HEADS")	=IF(B8="HEADS",1,0)+C7	=RAND()			
9	5	=IF(D9>$H$5,"TAILS","HEADS")	=IF(B9="HEADS",1,0)+C8	=RAND()			
10	6	=IF(D10>$H$5,"TAILS","HEADS")	=IF(B10="HEADS",1,0)+C9	=RAND()			
11	7	=IF(D11>$H$5,"TAILS","HEADS")	=IF(B11="HEADS",1,0)+C10	=RAND()			
12	8	=IF(D12>$H$5,"TAILS","HEADS")	=IF(B12="HEADS",1,0)+C11	=RAND()			
13	9	=IF(D13>$H$5,"TAILS","HEADS")	=IF(B13="HEADS",1,0)+C12	=RAND()			
14	10	=IF(D14>$H$5,"TAILS","HEADS")	=IF(B14="HEADS",1,0)+C13	=RAND()			
15	11	=IF(D15>$H$5,"TAILS","HEADS")	=IF(B15="HEADS",1,0)+C14	=RAND()			
16	12	=IF(D16>$H$5,"TAILS","HEADS")	=IF(B16="HEADS",1,0)+C15	=RAND()			
17	13	=IF(D17>$H$5,"TAILS","HEADS")	=IF(B17="HEADS",1,0)+C16	=RAND()			
18	14	=IF(D18>$H$5,"TAILS","HEADS")	=IF(B18="HEADS",1,0)+C17	=RAND()			
19	15	=IF(D19>$H$5,"TAILS","HEADS")	=IF(B19="HEADS",1,0)+C18	=RAND()			
20	16	=IF(D20>$H$5,"TAILS","HEADS")	=IF(B20="HEADS",1,0)+C19	=RAND()			
21	17	=IF(D21>$H$5,"TAILS","HEADS")	=IF(B21="HEADS",1,0)+C20	=RAND()			
22	18	=IF(D22>$H$5,"TAILS","HEADS")	=IF(B22="HEADS",1,0)+C21	=RAND()			
23	19	=IF(D23>$H$5,"TAILS","HEADS")	=IF(B23="HEADS",1,0)+C22	=RAND()			
24	20	=IF(D24>$H$5,"TAILS","HEADS")	=IF(B24="HEADS",1,0)+C23	=RAND()			
25							

Fig. 2.24 The formulae used in the tossing a coin model

When the spreadsheet is first set up, one set of random numbers is generated as the random number function is copied into column D. A new set of numbers can be generated by pressing the F9 key.

Activity

Set up a spreadsheet like this one. Compare the results with those you get by actually tossing a coin. How might you modify this model to simulate throwing a dice?

Another model using functions – examination results

An examining body, such as a GCSE board or a professional organisation, needs to keep a check on its examination results. After every examination session, the results need to be examined and compared with previous years to ensure that standards are being maintained. This is known as the process of moderation.

If, when all the marks are collected together, it is seen that the marks are much lower than usual, the examining body may decide that the examination was harder than normal. In this case, the board may decide to lower the marks needed to gain the different gradings. If the marks are all exceptionally high, the board may decide to raise the levels.

Figure 2.25 shows a spreadsheet which has been set up to look at the marks of some students.

The marks required for a Pass, Merit or Distinction are entered into cells E3, E4 and E5 respectively.

The marks gained by the students are entered into column B. A formula in column C looks at this mark and converts it into a grade. The formula in column C is:

=IF(B9>=$E$5,"Distinction", IF(B9>=$E$4,"Merit", IF(B9>=$E$3,"Pass", IF(B9<40,"Fail"))))

As you can see, it is another formula which uses the IF function, only this time there are several tests linked together. Notice the use of the absolute cell reference to the cells holding the marks needed for each grade.

The formula in column D is of the form:

=IF(C10="Distinction",1,0)+D9

This formula examines the grade in column C and enters a '1' in column D if the grade is a Distinction. The formulae in columns E, F and G work in a similar manner.

Activity

Make sure that you understand the formulae used in columns C and D. What are the formulae in columns E, F and G?

The formulae also total the numbers of Distinctions, Merits, Passes and Fails so that these figures can be entered into the cells at the top of the spreadsheet.

	A	B	C	D	E	F	G
3	**Number of Distinctions**		3	**Pass**	40		
4	**Number of Merits**		9	**Merit**	60		
5	**Number of passes**		11	**Distinction**	80		
6	**Number of fails**		2				
7							
8	**Student**	**Mark**	**Grade**	**Distinctions**	**Merits**	**Passes**	**Fails**
9	Student 1	46	Pass	0	0	1	0
10	Student 2	82	Distinction	1	0	1	0
11	Student 3	70	Merit	1	1	1	0
12	Student 4	65	Merit	1	2	1	0
13	Student 5	50	Pass	1	2	2	0
14	Student 6	53	Pass	1	2	3	0
15	Student 7	29	Fail	1	2	3	1
16	Student 8	56	Pass	1	2	4	1
17	Student 9	44	Pass	1	2	5	1
18	Student 10	75	Merit	1	3	5	1
19	Student 11	78	Merit	1	4	5	1
20	Student 12	49	Pass	1	4	6	1
21	Student 13	58	Pass	1	4	7	1
22	Student 14	52	Pass	1	4	8	1
23	Student 15	80	Distinction	2	4	8	1
24	Student 16	66	Merit	2	5	8	1
25	Student 17	23	Fail	2	5	8	2
26	Student 18	51	Pass	2	5	9	2
27	Student 19	63	Merit	2	6	9	2
28	Student 20	75	Merit	2	7	9	2
29	Student 21	73	Merit	2	8	9	2
30	Student 22	95	Distinction	3	8	9	2
31	Student 23	49	Pass	3	8	10	2
32	Student 24	61	Merit	3	9	10	2
33	Student 25	51	Pass	3	9	11	2
34							

Fig. 2.25 A spreadsheet showing student grades

Once the model has been set up, it is a simple matter to change the grade boundaries and see what effect this has on numbers of students achieving this grade. Figure 2.26 shows the effect of raising the marks required for each grade.

The models described here are all fairly simple examples. Spreadsheets can be used to model much more complex situations than these. However, whatever you are modelling it is very important to remember that what you are using is only a model and to bear in mind that you will have made assumptions when you set up the model and to treat the output accordingly.

	A	B	C	D	E	F	G
1	STUDENT GRADINGS						
2							
3	Number of Distinctions		1	Pass	45		
4	Number of Merits		9	Merit	65		
5	Number of passes		12	Distinction	85		
6	Number of fails		3				
7							
8	Student	Mark	Grade	Distinctions	Merits	Passes	Fails
9	Student 1	46	Pass	0	0	1	0
10	Student 2	82	Merit	0	1	1	0
11	Student 3	70	Merit	0	2	1	0
12	Student 4	65	Merit	0	3	1	0
13	Student 5	50	Pass	0	3	2	0
14	Student 6	53	Pass	0	3	3	0
15	Student 7	29	Fail	0	3	3	1
16	Student 8	56	Pass	0	3	4	1
17	Student 9	44	Fail	0	3	4	2
18	Student 10	75	Merit	0	4	4	2
19	Student 11	78	Merit	0	5	4	2
20	Student 12	49	Pass	0	5	5	2
21	Student 13	58	Pass	0	5	6	2
22	Student 14	52	Pass	0	5	7	2
23	Student 15	80	Merit	0	6	7	2
24	Student 16	66	Merit	0	7	7	2
25	Student 17	23	Fail	0	7	7	3
26	Student 18	51	Pass	0	7	8	3
27	Student 19	63	Pass	0	7	9	3
28	Student 20	75	Merit	0	8	9	3
29	Student 21	73	Merit	0	9	9	3
30	Student 22	95	Distinction	1	9	9	3
31	Student 23	49	Pass	1	9	10	3
32	Student 24	61	Pass	1	9	11	3
33	Student 25	51	Pass	1	9	12	3
34							

Fig. 2.26 A spreadsheet showing student grades with modified grade boundaries

Organisations and their use of information

The are many different sizes and types of organisation in our society. Some are formal organisations which are large and clearly structured, others are small and of a more informal nature.

Different organisations have different purposes. Some might be created to offer a product or service for sale with a view to making a profit. Some might provide charitable services and not create a profit.

There are other services that we might include, among them would be the vast array of health services, and the defence services of the army, navy, etc.

Table 2.5 Organisation classifications

Manufacturing	Selling goods	Selling services
Car manufacturers	Supermarkets	Banks
Builders	Chemists	Insurers
Farms	Newsagents	Airlines

Activity

What others can you think of? How would you categorise them? There are other categories than these mentioned above.

An organisation may be large or small, it may even be just one person, perhaps a plumber working for himself. The structure of an organisation will partly depend upon its size. A partnership of two or three people may not need a very formal internal communication method whereas a large multinational company will do. There are two methods of communication within an organisation, formal and informal. We shall look at the formal.

To help you understand some of the information about which we shall talk let us just have a quick look at the type of formal organisation structure that exists.

A large company will be divided up into more manageable units starting with areas of the business called 'functions'. Different organisations may call these functions by different names but they will be similar in purpose.

All organisations will have a **financial** function whether they be large or small, formal or informal in structure. There will be a **personnel** function if there are any employees at all. There will be a **sales** and **marketing** function, these may be together or separate depending upon the organisations needs. Such a formal organisation will have a **purchasing** function which may or may not be linked to a **production** function. Production will only occur where the primary purpose of the organisation is to manufacture goods, i.e. a car manufacturer will have a production function whereas a bank will not.

These companies lend themselves to a structure that is called '**hierarchical**' (see Figure 2.27). It will be in the form of a pyramid with information flowing up the organisation and instructions flowing down. At the very top of the pyramid are the directors or senior management. They will require information for different purposes than the bulk of the workforce at the base of the pyramid.

For example, senior management will be making tactical plans for the future, such as how to capture the market. Middle management will be looking to the practicalities of how these strategic objectives might be achieved, for instance, what advertising strategy might be effective and what the best products might be. The junior management and supervisors will ensure that the chosen advertising campaign is run, and that the product is created and available to customers, on a daily basis.

Fig. 2.27 Organisational hierarchy in a large company

Types of information

Each of these layers need different information to enable them to perform effectively. At the bottom of the pyramid is the operational information. This is needed to ensure that the organisation is meeting targets and actually performing. It will include details of sales for instance, which salesman sold what, when and to whom. This information is refined and passed up a level to the middle management. For example, instead of individual sales figures it will detail the whole department over the period in question. When we move up a level again then the information needed will be past performance of the whole of the organisation compared to targets, to competitors and projections of possible future performance.

So we have different types of information, strategic, tactical and operational. One for each of the management layers of the pyramid.

Another point to be remembered is that there are certain conditions that must be fulfilled for information to be called 'good' information. These are:

- **Timing**. Delays in the gathering and processing of data can result in potentially useful information becoming waste paper.
- **Appropriateness**. The information presented must be at the right level for the recipient and as up to date as necessary.
- **Accuracy**. The information must be sufficiently reliable for the user's purpose.
- **Detail**. The volume of detail to be stored and delivered must be suitable for the user's needs.
- **Frequency**. How often information is required is related to the timing. The preparation of final accounts is an activity that occurs once per year, but the payroll will be performed every month.
- **Understandability**. The information must be produced in such a way as to be understood by the recipient; the producer must, therefore, understand the recipient's needs.

The basic operational information is the most visible when you examine an organisation. It will be contained in many sources. Consider where information might be available:

- Product catalogues
- Order forms
- Sales invoices
- Delivery notes

All the above is operational information and it is used to enable the company to provide the service or sell the goods. The junior manager will send reports to the middle management. For example, giving details of the sales made during the report period by the individual salesmen in the company. The middle management will collate this information with similar data and present reports to senior management about how the company is performing.

Collecting data

So how is this data collected for all these reports? Let us look at an order processing system and see the operational data in use.

Remember the large mail order catalogues that we mentioned earlier? Initially goods were delivered to customers after a written order had been received. Nowadays, though this service is still available, increasingly orders are accepted over the telephone.

The customer registers with the company who will issue them with a unique identifying number.

Activity

Why do you suppose they do this? Why not just use the customer name to identify them?

This is used as an account number. When the customer wishes to purchase goods they phone in an order. This order will consist of certain data items. These are:

- Customer number
- Confirmation of customer name
- Confirmation of customer address
- Catalogue number (unique to each item type)
- Colour/size required
- Quantity required
- Item price

The company will have a number of operators whose job is to take orders over the telephone. The customer is asked for their customer number. The operator will key this into the computer system and receive a display showing the customer's name and address, which the operator will confirm with the customer. The customer is then asked for the order. They will give the item number, which the operator enters into the computer system. The system will display details of the goods on screen to the operator. These details include, for example, that the item is a T-shirt, the range of sizes and colours in which it comes, and the availability or otherwise of these colours and size combinations. The operator confirms the goods and item cost with the customer. The customer will then specify the quantity, colours and sizes they require. If the goods are not currently available the operator will advise the customer of any delay in supply and confirm the order still stands. The customer accepts or rejects the delivery and the contract is agreed.

We see from this that there is a lot of information being used in this small everyday transaction.

The customer has extracted the telephone number, and dialled it. The operator has announced who he or she is and the company name, then asked the caller to identify him or herself. The customer does so by use of their customer number. The customer number allows the operator to identify precisely which customer is calling. The customer will identify the goods they require to the operator by using the catalogue code(s). The customer passes on information as to how many, what size(s) and what colour(s). The operator will confirm to the customer that the goods are available or otherwise. The operator will ask the customer where the goods might be left should the delivery be attempted while the customer is out.

All this data together becomes the order. To recap let us list the data items on the complete order:

- Customer number
- Customer name
- Customer/delivery address
- Item code
- Item description
- Colour required
- Size
- Quantity required

The order sent in by ordinary post will consist of the same data items entered onto the preprinted order form. The relevant data items will be transferred onto the delivery note to allow the customer to confirm the items with their order. The invoice is a copy of the delivery note with the addition of the cost of the items and the total value of the order.

So we see that having data input using a keyboard from either a customer phone call or taken from a written form is a good method of data capture. There are many different forms used for this purpose and that might be used.

Activity

Can you think of any examples where data is captured on a form and later entered to a system using a keyboard?

Using a keyboard may not always be the best method to enter data. Consider a supermarket. What is the commonly used tool for data entry there? The till operators may use a laser device or other form of **bar code reader** to read the item code printed on the packaging.

Let us consider when a customer chooses to pay using a credit or debit card. The details of the account are held on the plastic card presented by the customer. The cashier swipes the card through a special **card reader**. The card reader is able to read the data contained in the magnetic strip on the reverse of the card. The cashier then enters the rest of the transaction details using a keypad.

The National Lottery uses very simple little forms to enable the players to select their numbers. These forms are then fed into a machine that reads the marks the player has made to register the selection. These **optical mark readers** are ideal for such simple data collection and input systems.

Another method of data entry that you may have seen used employs using a **concept keyboard**. These are increasingly used in restaurants and bars. The board is a flat pad with many sensitive areas; over this is laid a mat called an **overlay**. This overlay contains the names or codes of the different items on the menu or available drinks on each of the sensitive pads. The user simply touches these labelled areas and the software calculates the value of the bill. These save the user learning new prices when they change and increase the accuracy with which bills are calculated.

Structuring data

It might be that a report is required to show the total sales of individual lines of stock. This will be used to decide which items will be used in the next catalogue. If an item doesn't sell well then the management will not stock it.

Activity

How might such a report be laid out? What sort of data will be required to make it useful?

We can suggest that the company may wish to break down their sales by item line (see Table 2.6).

Table 2.6 Quarterly item sales (£)

	Quarter 1	Quarter 2	Quarter 3	Quarter 4
T-shirt TS123SD	12,345	12,379	85,563	95,123
Jacket KL532GT	95,486	85,632	45,623	12,365

Activity

Is this likely to be sufficiently detailed? It is more likely that some view will need to be seen of the sales by size of the items and the colours preferred. How would you lay out such a report?

Processing data

Data is processed in a number of ways to provide the useful information required. These processes include:

- Calculating
- Sorting
- Searching

Many of the reports that are required throughout an organisation will require calculations to be performed. We have talked about needing to know information about total sales, we therefore have a need to calculate these from the individual sale values.

How might a spreadsheet be used for this? You might set a spreadsheet out to calculate your income and expenditure.

Think of a telephone directory. Data is collected together and to make it easy to follow or use it is sorted. The telephone directory is sorted into alphabetical order by the surname of the owner of the telephone.

Activity

How would you find the number you need if it were all jumbled up in random order?

Having sorted the data for the telephone directory you will find it easy to search for the required number.

In a computerised data store it is not necessary to sort the data before searching. Searching will be done by the computer matching the data held to the details you specify. You may have a personal database listing all the numbers and details of friends, family and other contacts. Suppose you require to find a contact whose surname is Franco. You will enter a search such as, 'Surname = Franco'. The database will then search through the records looking at the field containing the surname data items and show any that contain a match for 'Franco'.

Storing information

The basic form in which data is stored in a computer is within a file. This file may be created by a spreadsheet or database package. The structure will be based upon the package. The database may be based upon several tables, each of which contains a number of records containing similar data items. For example, an organisation may have a database containing, among other data, a table of customer details – names, addresses, telephone numbers, etc.

We looked earlier at the spreadsheet which also stores information. This will be using the proprietary format of the spreadsheet package.

Every package has its own way of labelling files. You will give a file a name and the package will add an 'extension'. These three characters appear after the full stop in the filename.

Activity

Create a file in each of the packages available to you and save them. Look at your files. What extensions do you see listed? Can you identify the package that created the file?

Security procedures

Information technology is an essential part of the activities of many organisations, be they industrial, commercial or public. These organisations, use computer systems to store and process the data that is needed for their work. In many cases, the organisations could not function effectively without their computer systems. For example, international airlines could not handle the enormous volume of flights and passengers without their computerised booking systems. Large supermarkets are very dependent on their **Electronic Point of Sale** (EPOS) systems for checkout and stock control operations. Large chemical plants are monitored and controlled by central computer systems.

To these organisations, their information technology systems are a very valuable resource and the organisations will take steps to protect both the computer systems themselves and the data stored in the systems.

Many data handling systems store and process data about people, e.g. bank accounts, personnel records, medical records. The use of computers in this way places both moral and legal obligations on the organisations to protect the data. Individuals want to be sure that the information stored about them is accurate, is kept confidential and is not disclosed to people who have no right to see the information. The organisations have a moral obligation to protect the privacy of individuals and legal obligations under the terms of the **Data Protection Act** to ensure that the data they hold about people is both accurate and adequately protected.

Computer security involves protecting the hardware and software of a system against loss or damage and providing a means of recovering from any loss or damage that occurs. It also involves preventing unauthorised access to the data stored in a system. We will look at the methods used to protect both large centralised systems and small standalone systems.

Computer security centralised systems

Computer systems must be protected against physical hazards and errors that might cause loss or damage to equipment or stored data. Unauthorised access must also be prevented as this could also result in loss or damage and could compromise the confidentiality of the data held on the system.

Loss and damage

Computer hardware and the data on storage devices such as disks and tapes are vulnerable to several **physical hazards** such as:

- Theft
- Malicious damage
- Fire
- Flood
- Equipment failure
- Power failure

Computer equipment represents a valuable asset to an organisation and needs to be protected against the risk of **theft** or **malicious damage**. Central systems will normally be located in secure computer rooms. Access to these rooms will be restricted to the personnel who operate the computer and will be controlled by some type of security system such as code locks and magnetic stripe card locks on the doors. Many security systems record access to the computer room so that it is possible to trace who entered the room and the time of entry.

Fire is a hazard in computer installations. The equipment in a computer room generates quite a lot of heat and there are likely be considerable amounts of combustible material such as paper and magnetic tape in the room. Computer rooms should be protected by special fire extinguisher systems. These usually use a fire extinguishing gas called halon. Halon suffocates the fire and therefore it is important that staff are evacuated before the gas is released. Outside of working hours the system may be set to automatically release the gas in case of a fire.

Floods pose a serious risk to computer hardware and wiring. Computer rooms should not be situated in basements where flooding might be a problem. One flooding hazard arises because of the need to control the temperature in computer rooms, both to provide suitable working conditions for the computer operators and to prevent overheating of the equipment. This is usually done by means of water-cooled air conditioning units. If these units develop leaks, there is the risk of damage to equipment. Sensitive moisture detectors are usually installed in or on the floors of computer rooms to detect traces of moisture so that any leakage can be dealt with quickly.

Computer equipment such as disk and tape drives is subject to **failure** just like any other mechanical or electrical equipment. A faulty drive may damage the tape or disk and corrupt the data.

Power failure can damage equipment by causing read/write head crashes that damage disks and the data on them. Fluctuations in the power supply can cause loss of data. Power supplies to computer rooms should be protected by being on a separate circuit and being filtered to minimise fluctuations. Some organisations install battery backup systems for use in case of a complete power failure.

Data can also be lost or damaged because of **human error**. For example, a person may delete the wrong file or edit the wrong record in a database. It is not unknown for a disk to be reformatted by mistake, erasing all the data stored on it!

Activity

How can an organisation ensure that it will be able to recover from any loss or damage to its computer systems?

Damaged hardware is relatively easy to replace or repair. For example, a damaged disk can be removed from a disk drive and replaced with a new disk. Damage to data is more difficult to recover from, unless the organisation has implemented appropriate **backup** procedures.

Backing up data means taking copies of the files at regular intervals. With large systems, this usually means copying the files from the computer disks to tape. If backup copies of the files on a system are taken each night, it means that if a file is lost or damaged during the next day, the data can be restored to the state it was in at the beginning of the day, and only the day's work will be lost. It is important that the backup copies of the files are not stored in the computer room with the working copies of the files because if there were a fire, both copies would be lost. Backup copies should be stored away from the computer room, preferably in a fireproof safe or cabinet in another building. Both software and data files need to be backed up.

Activity

How will you back up your files? Where will you store your backup copies?

Organisations store and use data about people. For example, businesses hold information about their customers and their staff. Banks store details of their customers' accounts. The Inland Revenue holds information about our incomes. Doctors store medical records. The list is enormous. The data is stored to enable the organisations to function effectively.

Many people, however, are concerned about the amount of data that is held. They fear that their privacy is being eroded and that the data could be misused. People become concerned that too much personal data is held and that it can be accessed too easily, possibly by individuals who have no right to see the information. There are also concerns about the accuracy of stored data and that decisions about individuals may be made using information which is either incorrect or incomplete.

These concerns are recognised by governments and most countries have laws designed to protect the rights of the individual. The relevant law in the UK is the **Data Protection Act** which was passed in 1984, and amended in 1998.

The Data Protection Act applies to personal information, i.e. information about living, identifiable individuals. The 1984 Act only applied to information that was stored and processed by computer. Information that was held in paper files was not covered by the Data Protection Act. This was changed by the 1998 amendment.

Data held on computer may be subject to copyright legislation. As with books and other published items the ownership of the text belongs to either the author or the publisher. If you attempt to copy text from a computer based source, such as a CD-ROM containing an encyclopaedia, you will find the system downloads the statement of copyright.

The data collected by an organisation for its legal use actually belongs to that organisation. It is illegal for an employee to copy the data and pass it on or use it him- or herself as this would contravene the copyright laws.

Assessment evidence

This unit will be assessed by your tutor/assessor examining the work you place in your portfolio of evidence.

You will need to produce a relational database and a spreadsheet for your portfolio of evidence.

You must clearly identify the user needs, what do they require the applications to do for them? What data is to be processed within the applications you will create?

For the database consider how the data will be divided between the tables. Which data item will uniquely identify each record within each table? What data item(s) will create the relationship between the tables?

How will you design the spreadsheet? Where will the data be input?

Show how you enter and edit data. Show how you ensure the accuracy of the data. How do you verify the data? Does it exactly match your source? Is the data validated? Validated data is data which is likely to be correct. For example, there is no likelihood that someone was born on the 30 February.

By what criteria do you sort the data? Remember the telephone directory? By what criteria is the data in a telephone directory sorted?

Show how you search the data for specific record(s). Remember to collect and keep your printouts to show how you have met the requirements. You may decide to annotate (write notes on) these printouts to explain what they show.

Evaluate your database against the user needs. What did they need? How does your work enable them to do that? Is it easy to use? Are all your printouts clearly labelled? Do they make sense to you and your user?

You will need to provide a spreadsheet to meet user needs. These needs must be clearly identified by yourself in your description. You should include and identify where you have used:

- Suitable row heights
- Column widths
- Cell formats
- Cell references
- Arithmetic functions and formulae
- IF. . .THEN statements

Again there should be annotated printouts, clearly labelled to identify what they are for and what they show.

You must keep backups and demonstrate how you have ensured the accuracy of the data.

You will need to evaluate your work against the user needs, showing how it provides the necessary functions and suits the purposes. You should also be able to suggest improvements that you would make in the future or if you started the piece again.

Figure 2.28 gives the criteria which needs to be met to achieve a Pass, Merit or Distinction.

Pass	Merit	Distinction
To achieve a pass your work must show:	To achieve a merit your work must show:	To achieve a distinction your work must show:
• Clear descriptions of the user's needs, the information to be processed and the processing required.	• Effective use of software to sort on multiple fields, make use of cell relationships and produce good quality printed copy, showing both data content, formats and formulae (clear and detailed annotation, screen prints or notes must explain why and how all printed items are produced).	• An in-depth understanding of database and spreadsheet systems and an evaluation of your work making suggestions for improvement and describing any problems experienced.
• Table structures created using suitable field names, field lengths, data types, primary keys and relations.	• Good use of titles, graphic lines, spacing, text size, text enhancement, column and row headers, page headers or footers and graph labels to enhance the presentations, making them attractive, easy to read and free of layout errors.	• Your ability to use technical language fluently and produce clear, coherent and comprehensive explanations and annotations.
• Suitable spreadsheets created using row heights, column widths, cell formats, titles, cell references, IF ... THEN statements, arithmetic functions and formulae are created and used.	• You have checked your work for accuracy and corrected obvious errors.	• Effective and efficient use of complex search criteria on related tables, formulae and absolute cell references to produce the desired outcomes.
• Your ability to use data-processing skills to enter data, sort, search, calculate, predict results, produce different types of charts or line graphs and create printed reports using related tables.	• Your ability to work independently to produce your work to agreed deadlines by carrying out your work plans effectively.	• A constructive evaluation of your documents that identifies good and less good features, suggests possible improvements to them and compares them with standards used by organisations.
• You have produced printed copy showing that you have met the above requirements and explaining your work (this may include screen prints or annotated data output).	• Clear progression from the design stage to completion and evaluation.	
• Your ability to check the accuracy of your data and keep backup copies of files.		

The above criteria only need to be met once for this unit. Except where otherwise stated, they may be met in either your database or your spreadsheet.

Fig. 2.28 Unit 2 Handling Information – grade descriptors

Unit 3

HARDWARE AND SOFTWARE

Introduction

Hardware

Storage devices

Output devices

Software

Applications software

Computer programming

Standard ways of working

Assessment evidence

Introduction

This unit is about the nuts and bolts of the computer, all the parts that go together to make this useful tool that is so much part of life in the twenty-first century. In this unit you will learn to:

- Understand ICT specifications for hardware and software
- Select an ICT system
- Configure an ICT system to meet the needs of users
- Write a macro to improve efficient use of application software
- Write a program to display hypertext information using hypertext markup language (HTML)
- Understand and develop good practice in your use of ICT

The material you covered in Unit 1, Presenting Information, and Unit 2, Handling Information, will help you in this unit. In creating your hypertext presentation you will have a further opportunity to apply the good presentation techniques you learned in Unit 1.

The main topics you will cover here are:

- Hardware
- Software
- Computer programming
- Macro programs
- Hypertext markup language (HTML) programs
- Standard ways of working

Hardware

What is hardware? Many of you will be familiar with hardware but may not recognise it as such. Consider the machines with which you are familiar. Do any have keyboards, joysticks, mice, printers, display screens? All these items are known as hardware.

Hardware may be defined as all those parts of a machine that can be touched. We can further divide hardware into the following areas:

- Input devices
- Processor unit
- Output devices
- Cables and connectors

Input devices

Before data can be processed it must be entered into the computer in a form that the machine will understand. Computers are electronic machines and cannot understand the wide vocabulary that we enjoy in our speech and written words.

Input devices are those parts of a computer system that allow the user to either communicate with the computer or to enter into the computer the data that the program requires.

With what input devices are you familiar? A wide range of input devices are available, many more than we can outline in this unit. Let us look at a few.

Keyboard

The design of a standard computer keyboard is based upon that developed for the typewriter. It is often referred to as a QWERTY keyboard. It is so called because these are the first keys on the top left hand side of the top row of the keyboard on which this is based. The keys were arranged in this way to slow down the original typists. (See Figure 3.1.)

The keys have various characters represented upon them, including:

- The alphabet
- Number keys (both above the alpha keys and on the numeric keypad)
- Punctuation marks
- Function keys

The 'function' keys will have a variety of purposes depending on the needs of the user. The common standard keyboard will also include a separate numeric keypad and a group of keys to control the movement of the cursor (an indicator used to locate the next item of text input).

As the user presses a key on the keyboard, a code representing that particular key is sent to the **central processing unit** (this is explained later in this section), which processes the keystroke and if required 'looks' for the next code. The codes are constructed in a numeric form known as **binary**. This is a simple set of zeros and ones (more later).

Activity

See if you can find out why a typewriter designer would want to slow a keyboard operator down. If you were to develop a keyboard how would you order the keys?

Concept keyboards

There are some circumstances in which the standard keyboard is not suitable. To provide access to data input the concept keyboard was developed. These are available in situations where a full QWERTY board is not convenient, e.g. in education for very young children or in busy restaurants and bars.

The boards have sensitive areas like pads. The user has an overlay, a plastic or paper sheet on which are marked the 'values' ascribed to these pads. These overlays can be changed depending on the application being run. (An application is the purpose for which the machine is used, for example, the application used to write this book is called a word processor.)

Also available are other touch sensitive keypads which are ideally suited for those circumstances where there is no need for a complex series of inputs to be available, for example computerised lathes, ATMs (Automated Teller Machines, also known as cash machines).

Activity

Can you find any other areas that use concept keyboards?

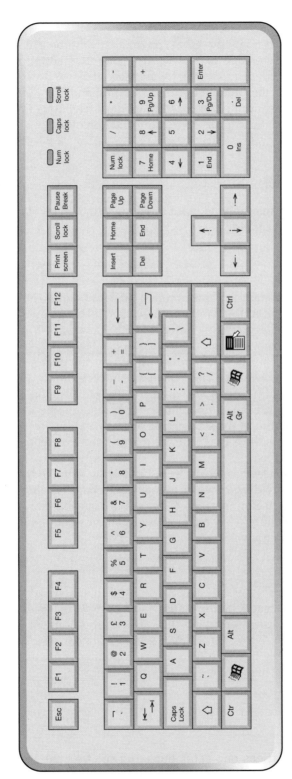

Fig. 3.1 A standard computer keyboard

Microphone

Microphones can accept verbal commands from the user. They are beginning to be used beyond the areas of broadcasting and other sound recording and production. With the advent of modern software (see later) we now have the facility to dictate text to the machine and give correction commands.

Microphone input is also used in modern telephone information systems such as those available for various Tourist Information offices.

Activity

Can you find microphone input used anywhere else? What are the restrictions on using sound as input?

Mouse

The mouse is a familiar and common piece of equipment with most PCs. This object fits in the palm of the hand and has a small ball located in its base. The object we now call a mouse was first patented in 1970 as 'an X-Y position indicator for a display system'.

As the user pushes the mouse around on the desk surface the cursor on screen matches its movements. Thus, the user can very simply and easily control the cursor. The movement of the mouse on the desktop rolls a ball against two rollers, set at right angles to each other. One roller translates the movement to a value for X (across the width of the screen), the other to a value for Y (the height of the screen). This then gives the XY co-ordinate that the software will translate to a specific location on the screen.

The mouse also has two or three buttons on its top edge, which the user 'clicks' to cause menus to drop down or to make on-screen selections. The user may, by 'clicking and dragging', move objects around the screen. Many applications depend upon the use of a mouse. They are most useful in the operation of graphical user interfaces (GUIs), e.g. Windows ™.

Trackball

This is an alternative to the mouse and as simple to use. It does not require any extra desk space as the user rotates the ball with their fingers. It also has buttons to indicate selection. If you have never seen a trackball, turn a standard mouse upside down! The way in which the trackball operates is identical to that explained above for the mouse, it is another 'X-Y position indicator'.

Activity

Look in magazines and catalogues and see how the trackball compares with the mouse. Which is the dearest? Why do you think that is?

Joystick

The joystick may be familiar to those of you that play computer or arcade games. These are a miniature version of the joystick a pilot uses to control a jet.

The sensors that are used to 'feel' the movement are located at the base of the stick. The operational buttons are found on the head of the stick and, in games, may be used to 'fire' weapons. The overall function is very similar to the mouse or trackball, allowing scrolling, selecting, dragging and dropping, etc.

Scanners

Scanners are increasingly used to transfer images and text from paper into a computer. They code the image according to the density of light and shade. The result may then be viewed on screen by a package that handles bitmap files.

Specialised scanners include **optical mark readers** (OMRs), **optical character readers** (OCRs) and **bar code readers**.

OMRs makes use of preprinted documents on which the data is marked by means of a pencil stroke across the relevant boxes. The pencil lead is made of a substance called graphite. This completes an electrical circuit when the reading mechanism 'brushes' over the document. This was essential for the older OMRs, however, modern technology moves on and now they operate if the marks are completed in ballpoint pen, e.g. those used in The National Lottery terminals.

OCR devices read stylised printed characters. There are a number of designs of such characters (these designs are called a font). The OCR reflects light off the characters and converts them into digital patterns for comparison with the stored character set.

With these computerised readers the reject rates are less than 10 per cent and error rates are less than 1 per cent. However, this assumes that the documents are kept 'clean', for example OMR documents must not be creased or folded as this renders it very difficult for the machine to read them. The speed of input from these forms is between 100 and 1,500 documents per minute.

We are all familiar with bar code readers commonly used in the retail industry. It is almost impossible to buy any goods today that are not labelled with a bar code. The thickness of the bars and their spacing provides a meaningful code. The reader may be in the form of a wand or pen that is run over the printed bar code, alternatively the goods themselves may be passed over a screen in a desk. The reader will compare the code it has read with those held in memory and extract the price details, etc. These allow shops to keep very accurate stock records and do analyses of sales. Customers like the detailed till receipts that are available.

Other common scanners are the 'flat bed' scanners which are often sold as part of home PCs. These enable the user to place a document on the bed, a glass screen similar to a photocopier. The lid is put down and the machine 'scans' across the document, creating an image.

The digital image can then be stored on a computer and further manipulated using appropriate software. If it is a graphic then painting or drawing packages may be used. If the document contains text then it may be read into a word processor using suitable optical character recognition software. The results will vary depending on the quality of the original document.

Activity

Look in computing magazines and search on the Internet to see what other scanners there are available. For what purposes might they be used?

Digital cameras

These are rapidly coming down in price and are increasingly available to all and not just professionals.

As with the 35mm camera with which you may be familiar, these have a lens through which the image is focussed. However, unlike the 35mm camera, the image is not focused onto light sensitive film but onto an array of light sensitive transistors. Each picture element (pixel) consists of a red, a blue and a green transistor. This is called a **charge coupled device** (CCD).

Activity

Why are the transistors sensitive to red, blue and green light? What about all the other colours of the spectrum? How are they created?

These transistors generate an analogue electrical current. An analogue current is a continuous and varying current. This needs to be converted into the digital data which can be understood by the computer. Passing the current through an **analogue to digital converter** (ADC) does this.

The digital data is then sent to a **digital signal processor** (DSP) for the contrast and detail to be adjusted. The DSP then compresses the image (much as any digital file may be compressed) before sending it to the storage medium.

At the time of writing cameras cost as little as £150 (and prices are falling all the time). However, as with all such equipment, the quality will vary, often in line with the price.

Activity

Using magazines and photographic shops find out how much digital cameras cost today. Who might use them? Where might they be useful in a commercial environment?

Sensors

We are all familiar with sensors in our everyday life, so much so that perhaps they are ignored. For example, the fridge has a sensor that measures the temperature, which is compared to that set by the user. If the sensor shows a higher value than the setting the motor is switched on. The motor operates a pump that moves cooling fluid around the system. When the sensor registers a value lower than that set the motor is switched off.

Sensors may be used to input data into a microcomputer. These are widely used in all sorts of domestic, commercial and industrial situations. These may measure light, temperature, contact or sound.

Activity

You have been given an example of sensors in use in a domestic situation. Where might they be employed in a commercial and an industrial environment? What would the sensors measure?

Main processor unit

This is the heart of any machine. Let us start by looking at a typical machine. The external appearance of a main processor unit is shown in Figure 3.2.

The front panel will usually have an ON/OFF switch, one or more disk drive slots and indicator lights for mains power and the disk drives.

Compare Figure 3.2 with a machine you know. There may be some differences. Like cars, they all do much the same using the same technology but there are many different models and makes.

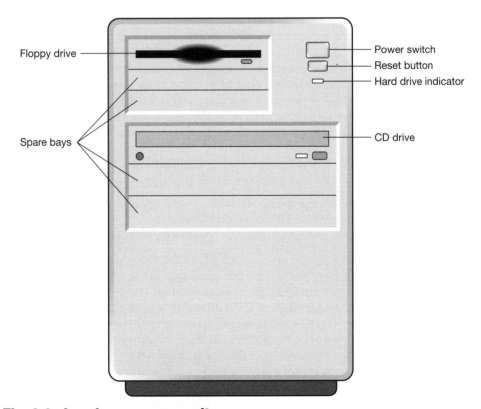

Fig. 3.2 A main processor unit

The rear panel has a fan and sockets, or ports, to connect mains power and peripheral devices such as the monitor, keyboard, mouse, printer and microphone. These ports may be labelled with pictures of the appropriate devices to help the user to connect the system together (see 'cables and connectors' on page 117).

Now let's look inside. First we remove the cover of the processor unit to reveal the power supply, disk drives and the circuit boards of the system. A set of cables links the various parts together.

Activity

You need to see inside a real machine for your studies. Some will have all cables neatly tied in place, others may look as if a plate of spaghetti has been dumped in the case. Which is the better? If you were an engineer and needed to repair or replace part of the equipment, which would you prefer to find? Would you include this in a guide to 'good practice'?

The power supplied from the mains is what is known as 'alternating current' (AC). This is not suitable for use by the machine. The incoming AC is converted by the power supply equipment to the precisely controlled 'direct current' (DC) voltages that are needed by the computer's electronic components. The power supply unit also contains a fan. The fan prevents the machine from overheating due to the high density of components. The disk drives are used to store data permanently.

Depending on the type of PC you are looking at, there will be one or more circuit boards. The flat circuit board covered with chips at the bottom of the main processor unit is the system board or motherboard. This board is a glass fibre sheet which has a conducting track etched on it that connects the various chips together.

The external appearance of a chip unit is usually a square or rectangular piece of plastic with pins to plug the chip to the board. The chip itself is much smaller and consists of a complex electronic circuit produced on a piece of silicon. Figure 3.3 shows a circuit board with many chips on it. The chip unit at the bottom of the board has a window in it, through which the chip itself and its connecting wires are visible.

The motherboard carries some essential components:

- A central processor chip, which performs most of the work
- Memory chips which are used to store data
- Chips which are used to control peripherals, such as disk drives and monitors

The most important chip in a PC is the microprocessor. Almost every piece of data that enters or leaves the machine passes through this chip to be either processed or redirected. Because of its importance, this chip is given the name of **central processing unit**, or CPU. Many PCs in use today use one of the chips made by Intel or AMD Processors. We have recently seen an enormous growth in the speed and power of these chips, at the time of writing a fairly standard machine is being sold for the home user featuring chips with a speed of 750MHz (see below).

The microprocessor contains a clock generator which is used to synchronise the entire operation of the machine. The clock generator produces regular pulses, at a rate of between 16 and 100 million cycles per second. This is usually expressed in

Fig. 3.3 A circuit board with chips

MHz (megahertz or million cycles per second) and sets an upper limit to the speed at which the processor may function, so this determines the effective speed of the PC. When you buy a PC, the processor is usually specified in terms of the chip and its speed. For example, a PC may be described as containing a Pentium III processor running at 933MHz or perhaps an AMD Athlon running at 950MHz.

Activity

Look at adverts in the press to see what is available today.

The motherboard also carries memory chips which are used to store either data or programs. This memory is referred to as random access memory or RAM. In older machines these RAM chips are groups of chips attached to a card which plugs into the motherboard. These cards are known as **single in-line memory modules** or SIMMs. More modern machines use forms of **dual in-line memory modules** (DIMMs). These are larger in data terms than the older SIMMs. Most PCs in use today have a minimum of 64MB of RAM.

Activity

Look in catalogues, magazines and any shops available to you. How much does it cost to upgrade a PC by the addition of more RAM?

As mentioned earlier, the processor unit may contain more than one circuit board. Many machines will have boards plugged into the motherboard which control the video display and the disks, although in some machines these functions are integrated into the motherboard. Additional boards, known as expansion cards, may be needed to connect the PC to a communications network or to provide sound for some applications. These additional boards plug into the motherboard.

Many computer users today need to connect to other computers. This is called networking and may be done by linking the machines directly using a cable, or by telephone.

If the machines are linked by cable the motherboard will need a **network interface card** (NIC) installing. This will control the way in which the computers 'talk' to each other.

If the computer needs to use the telephone line then another card is needed called a **mo**dulator **dem**odulator (**modem**). This converts the digital 'language' of the computer into the analogue form that is still common to telephone communications.

Memory

The processing power of the computer depends on its ability to store vast amounts of information and to access this information rapidly.

We need to consider how computers store data. Computers are digital and electronic in their operation. All the programs and data are stored in code using zeros or ones. This is called binary code. Each **b**inary dig**it** is called a **bit**. This is the smallest data item that the computer will hold.

A series of eight bits is called a **byte**. Each byte may contain the code to represent one character of the alphabet. For example, in the American Standard Code for Information Interchange (ASCII) the character 'A' is represented by the code 01000001.

Remember we said that memory is measured in bytes.

1 kilobyte or 1KB	=	1024 bytes	=	2^{10} bytes
1 megabyte or 1MB	=	1024 Kbytes	=	2^{20} bytes
1 gigabyte or 1GB	=	1024 Mbytes	=	2^{30} bytes
1 terabyte or 1TB	=	1024 Gbytes	=	2^{40} bytes

There are two main categories of computer storage. The main memory, also known as **random access memory**, or RAM, and **read only memory**, known as ROM.

RAM is used to store programs and the necessary data while the programs are being run. This form of storage is also referred to as the main store, primary store or immediate access store. When the power is switched off any data and programs stored in RAM are lost.

Longer term storage makes use of hardware devices such as disks and tapes. This type of storage is referred to as the secondary store, auxiliary store or backing store.

Earlier we said that memory consists of a series of chips on the motherboard. Remember there are two types of memory chip.

Random access memory or RAM is memory that can be written to and read from. RAM is best thought of as a kitchen work surface. It is the area where all data is processed, similar to the food preparation area in a kitchen. All the work of the machine is stored in RAM. RAM will be used during the transfer of data between the main processing unit and peripherals, such as printers and screens. Look at the advertisements for PCs in a suitable magazine. You will see that most machines offered for sale are advertised as having between 64MB and 256MB of RAM.

Activity

List the amounts of RAM offered with machines. Not so very many years ago the average machine was sold with 4MB of RAM, this could be upgraded to 8MB. What do you notice about the numbers?

ROM is memory which can only be read. It is a non-volatile form of memory so the contents are not lost when the computer is switched off. An initial routine, stored in ROM, called the bootstrap loads the operating system (see page 132) into RAM. Included in ROM will be some utility programs that are part of the operating system.

Cables and connectors

You will hear ports referred to as being either **parallel** or **serial**. A parallel port is one in which the bits making up each byte of data are transmitted simultaneously along parallel wires in a cable. Parallel ports usually have connectors that have 25 pins. Parallel ports are generally used for connecting printers.

A serial port transmits data a bit at a time along a single wire. Serial ports are used to connect devices such as modems, mice and printers that can operate in serial mode.

The rear panel of the main processing unit also has the covers for the expansion slots. These are used if an extra unit such as a communications board needs to be added to the system.

We are increasingly seeing PCs that are equipped with a new type of connector called the **universal serial bus** (USB). This is a new peripheral connection that is designed to replace the wide variety currently in use. These will include the mouse, keyboard, monitor, parallel, serial buses, etc. The USB will enable up to 127 devices to be simultaneously attached to the PC. At the time of writing many machines are coming fitted with either a USB port or hub, although not as wide a variety of peripherals are available.

Activity

Using appropriate magazines, catalogues and other sources look at the advertisements. Are USBs offered as a feature of new machines? Can you find suitable hardware that will make use of them? Are they more or less expensive than non-USB hardware?

Storage devices

These may be viewed as both input and output devices. We have mentioned the use of ROM for the bootstrap, the code that tells the machine it is to be a computer and where to find the software that will help it to perform. We also talked of the 'work surface' that is RAM. This is where the majority of work is held during the processing of data. We will now look at a few of the devices and methods available to write and rewrite data we wish to keep when the machine is switched off.

Remember that RAM is said to be **volatile** and that means it cannot be used for this. In order to be stored permanently, data must be copied from the memory of the computer to some other form of storage. This is called **backing store**. Material stored on backing store is arranged into **files**. A file might be a computer program, a word processing document or a file of data such as an accounts file.

The different types of backing store are classified according to the method of reading. The data may be accessed either **serially** or **directly**.

A serial access store is one in which all the data has to be read in sequence. Magnetic tape is the most common type of serial access store. To reach a file stored on tape, the whole tape must be read from the beginning until you reach the required file. This is similar to audio magnetic tape. If you wish to listen to a particular musical track you have to wind through the tape until you reach it – you cannot jump directly to it.

A direct access store is one in which any data item or file can be accessed directly. An example of a direct access device is the CD-ROM. If you wish to listen to a particular track on a CD you can jump directly to it.

There are a number of readily available storage devices, we shall look at a few:

- Magnetic disk
- CD-ROM
- DVD
- Magnetic tape

Magnetic disks

Most PCs use two types of magnetic disks – floppy disks and hard disks. Floppy disks are small, removable disks which slot into a disk drive which is accessible on the front of the main processor unit. Hard disks are devices which usually reside inside the main processor unit. Some laptop computers have removable hard disk units for security reasons.

Figure 3.4 shows two floppy disks, one of 5¼ inches and one of 3½ inches, together with a CD-ROM disk.

Floppy disks

Floppy disks may be familiar to you. They are made of a plastic disk coated with an iron oxide to give a magnetisable surface. The data is stored in the binary codes mentioned earlier, small areas of the disk are set to either north or south polarity, representing either zero or one.

The disk is contained within a protective case. Two sizes are generally used, with diameters of 5¼ inches and 3½ inches respectively. The cover of the 5¼ is a stiff card while that of the 3½ is of plastic. The 5¼ is seldom used today; the 3½ is very common.

The data is recorded onto the disk around a series of **concentric tracks** (see Figure 3.5). Each track is further divided into **sectors** each of which are separated by **inter-**

Fig. 3.4 Computer disks and a CD-ROM

sector gaps. The size of the sector is limited to that amount of data that may be read from or written to the disk in one operation.

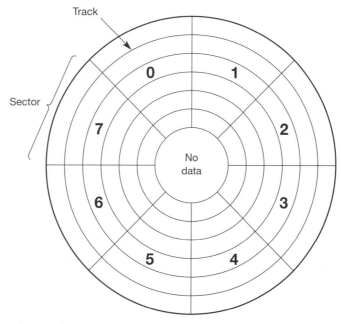

Fig. 3.5 Tracks and sectors on a formatted disk

Formatting a disk divides it into these tracks and sectors. The amount that may be stored on a floppy disk depends on whether one or two sides of the disk are used and how many tracks and sectors there are. Modern 3½ inch disks normally have 80 tracks and a capacity of 1.44MB, whereas the older style 5¼ inch disks used to have 40 or 80 tracks and storage capacities of 360KB or 1.2MB of data.

Because the 3½ inch floppy disk has a rigid plastic case it is slightly stronger than the 5¼ inch disk. Also, the exposed surface of the disk is protected by a metal cover when it is not in use. The 3½ inch disk drive uses a spindle mechanism to spin the disk at a speed of about 360rpm. The spindle fits into the square hole in the metal centre of the disk. The larger notch is used to determine the start of the tracks to assist in the location of data. To read from or write to the disk the mechanism uses **read/write heads**. These heads touch the disk surface through the gap in the sleeve. This is why you must be careful never to insert or remove a floppy disk while the disk drive light is on.

As with most recording media there is a **write protect notch** which determines whether it is permissible to write data to the disk or erase information from it. The write protect mechanism consists of a small hole in the corner of the disk with a sliding cover. When the notch is open, data can be written to the disk. If the notch is closed by the sliding cover it is not possible to write to the disk or alter the data on it, although the data on the disk can be read. A disk with a closed notch is said to be write protected.

The 5¼ inch disk is operated in a very similar manner to the 3½ disk. It has a central hole for the mechanism to spin the disk, together with an index hole for locating the start of tracks. There is a hole in the cover to enable the read/write heads to access the disk. There is also a write protection mechanism whereby the open notch enables data to be written to the disk. However, if the notch is covered the disk is protected from such activities.

Floppy disks are fairly robust, but they should still be handled and stored carefully. When they are not in use they should be kept in a suitable disk box to protect them. You should never touch the exposed magnetic surface of the disk because fingerprints attract dust which can cause damage to the disk surface and the read/write heads. Disks should also be protected from extremes of temperature and stray magnetic fields which can corrupt the data stored on the disk.

Floppy disks are used to store data and to transfer information between computers. Software is sometimes supplied on floppy disks. If you share computers with others you will probably store your work on your own disks so that you can keep it safe. Another important use of floppy disks is to make backup copies of files stored on the hard disk of a system. Backing up files is very important. You should always keep more than one copy of important files and store one copy in a safe place away from the computer.

Hard disks

Hard disks for microcomputers are rigid disks which are built into sealed units which reside inside the main processing unit. They are not usually removable. A disk unit may contain one disk or several disks stacked above each other. The disks are made of aluminium with a diameter of around 5¼ inches and are coated on both sides with a magnetic material. There is a read/write head for each surface of the

Fig. 3.6 An opened hard disk drive showing the read/write heads and platters

disk. The read/write heads float just above the surfaces of the disk and all move together as part of a head assembly.

Figure 3.6 shows a hard disk drive which has been opened to show the disks and the read/write heads.

Each surface is formatted with tracks and sectors in the same way as a floppy disk (see Figure 3.5). In use, the disk spins at a high speed. To access a particular sector on the disk, the heads move across the disk until they are over the required track. The heads then remain still and the required sector is read as it passes the read/write heads.

The read/write heads are mounted very close to the disk surfaces and actually float on a cushion of air created by the movement of the disk. The gap between the disk surface and the heads is so small that a speck of dust can cause a '**head crash**', damaging the disk and head and destroying the data on the disk. For this reason, the disk units are completely sealed to prevent contamination with moisture or dust.

Hard disks provide very fast access to large amounts of data. At the time of writing storage capacities of hard disks used in PCs range from about 7.6GB to 30GB. Hard disks are used to store operating systems and applications software and user files. As access times are fast, much faster than floppy disks, many users like to store their working files on the hard disk. However, if this is done, it is important that backup copies of files are stored on floppy disk, so that if a head crash does occur, all the data will not be lost.

Hard disks are also used extensively for data storage on mainframe systems. They are generally much larger and have greater storage capacities. Hard disks for mainframe systems are often in the form of exchangeable disk packs, so that the disks are not fixed in the drive but can be taken out and replaced by another disk or pack.

CD-ROM

CD-ROM stands for **Compact Disk Read Only Memory**. Most people will be familiar with the audio compact disk. The same technology can be used to store large amounts of computer data. A CD-ROM disk is 12cm in diameter and holds about 650MB of data. The data on a CD-ROM disk is stored in the form of tiny pits in the surface of the disk. The disk is read by focusing a laser beam on the surface of the disk as it revolves. The light is reflected from the surface and the pattern of pits can be read.

CD-ROM disks have a protective plastic coating which enables them to be handled without damaging the data which is recorded on the disk. CD-ROM drives are available for use with most microcomputers and can be installed in the main processor unit.

The storage capacity of the CD-ROM makes it a very suitable medium for storing large reference works such as encyclopaedias. Multimedia systems make a great deal of use of CD-ROM to store text, voice, music, video and photographs. Application software is also supplied on CD-ROM.

The information on a CD-ROM disk is placed on the disk when it is manufactured – it cannot be altered or added to by the user.

Another type of CD is the **CD-R**, a writeable CD. It is possible to get a drive that will not only read CDs but also write them. Using a specially prepared blank disk it is possible to write your own CDs, either audio or data. You may choose this as the means for backing up data if the volumes are too great for floppy disks.

A form of optical disk which can be written to is the **write once read many** or **WORM** disk. These disks have a similar appearance to a CD-ROM disk but have a greater storage capacity – around 1000MB. (CD-ROM disks have a lower capacity because they are mass produced.) WORM disks have a surface which is coated with a film of a non-metallic substance called tellurium. A laser beam is used to burn the pits into the surface of the film. Once data has been written to disk it cannot be erased – the disk can be written to once, but the data can be read many times. WORM disks are used to back up files which may need to be stored for a long time. WORM disks are also used by multimedia developers.

Erasable optical disks or **magneto-optical disks** are another development. The disks are similar in appearance to a floppy disk, being in a case which looks like that used for a 3½ inch floppy disk. There are, however, different physical sizes depending upon the system chosen. Disk capacities are around 200MB.

The surface of an erasable optical disk is made of a special alloy. Instead of burning a pattern onto the disk surface, the laser beam heats spots on the disk surface allowing magnetic molecules in the alloy surface to be aligned by a magnetic field. When the spot cools, the magnetic pattern becomes fixed and can only be changed by reapplying heat. The data can therefore be deleted and rewritten when required. As with the other types of optical disk, a lower power laser beam is used to read the data from the disk.

DVD

DVD means **digital versatile disk**. This is still relatively new technology in the UK, although widely accepted in the US where it is to be found in the home cinema market.

Physically the DVD looks very similar to the standard CD. However, they are very different. Where the CD stores 650MB of data the DVD-ROM can store up to 17GB. With modern hard drives the size they are this is clearly attractive to those who wish to back up their data.

DVDs store data as a set of tiny pits within the disk structure. To increase the volume of data stored these pits had to be made much smaller and placed more closely together than those on the standard CD. To allow this more closely packed data to be read a new thinner laser beam was also developed. This enabled the new disks to hold 4.7GB. This wasn't enough to enable their use with films, as it only allowed two hours of compressed video to be stored. Although sufficient for some films others would require more space.

The solution was a disk with dual layers – a semi-transparent gold layer with another positioned beneath it. The second layer is bonded to the first with a special resin that allows laser light to pass through. The laser reads the top gold layer first and then transfers to the lower layer.

DVD-RAM is slightly different in that it can only contain 2.6GB on a single-sided disk and 5.2GB on a double-sided disk at the time of writing. It is anticipated that these will be used by companies that need to master disks for mass production.

Activity

Using current magazines and the Internet compare the prices of CD-RW (CD read/write) drives and those for reading DVD-ROM.

Magnetic tape

Magnetic tape is an inexpensive serial access backing storage medium which can be used with both microcomputers and mainframes.

Figure 3.7 shows a tape drive. To maintain even tension, loops of the tape fall into semi-vacuum chambers. The level of these loops is monitored by the tape level sensors. The tape only moves in one direction past the read/write heads for reading and writing.

Two formats are used with microcomputers: tape cassettes and tape cartridges.

Standard tape cassettes have been used to store computer data, and software for some early home computers was supplied on these cassettes. However, transferring data to and from a tape cassette is very slow.

Tape cartridges are larger than standard tape cassettes and are often used in tape streamers – a unit which is used to back up the contents of a hard disk.

Output devices

These are items of hardware that produce the results of the processing. It may be the monitor on which you view your document, or the paper copy of your document, or even the sound of the music you composed.

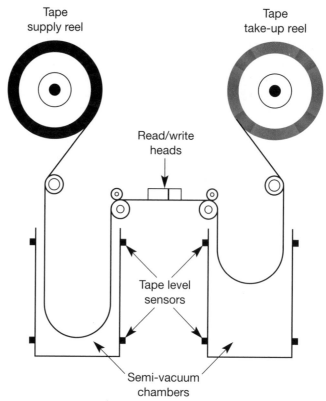

Tape
supply reel

Tape
take-up reel

Read/write
heads

Tape level
sensors

Semi-vacuum
chambers

Fig. 3.7 A tape drive

Monitors

The computer screen or monitor is probably the most important output device you will use. Another name for the screen is visual display unit or VDU.

The screen is an integral part of the standalone microcomputer. This is because microcomputers are used interactively. For example, if you are using a word processing package, you enter data by typing on the keyboard. As you press the keys, the characters are displayed on the screen. Any changes you make in your document, either by pressing keys or by using the mouse are immediately shown on the screen. You are interacting with the system all the time you are using it – inputting data and responding to the output. This interaction would be impossible without the screen.

Figure 3.8 shows a typical monitor. Monitors come in many sizes. The size can be expressed in either inches or centimetres but is always the diagonal length. The diagonal measurement of a monitor may be 19 inches. However, the visible area of the screen is smaller than the advertised size as the monitor is in a case, the frame of which reduces the screen size. Therefore, a 19 inch monitor may only have 17 inches in view.

Activity

What size monitors do you have available to use?

Fig. 3.8 A typical monitor

Controls are provided to allow the user to adjust the brightness and contrast of the display to comfortable levels, similar to a television. Larger monitors are available for applications such as computer aided design and desktop publishing where large and very detailed displays are needed.

Most modern microcomputer systems use monitors that display the output in colour. Some older systems, and often monitors used as terminals to central systems, display the output in monochrome. This means that the data is displayed in one colour or tone on a background that is a different colour or tone. Examples are white text/graphics on a black background or light green text/graphics on a darker green background.

Activity

Can you find somewhere that uses a monochrome screen?

The clarity of the picture on the screen depends on the resolution of the monitor, which may be defined as having high resolution, medium resolution or low resolution. The resolution of a monitor is measured in **pixels** (pixels is an abbreviation of picture elements).

The entire screen is divided into these small picture elements or pixels. Each of these areas may be changed as required to produce an image. These changes will include shades of light and dark or colour. This is done in a similar manner to the dots of a dot matrix printer. The **resolution** of the screen is determined by the number of pixels, the higher the number of pixels the higher the resolution.

Most PCs used today have a high resolution screen which displays at least 640 × 400 pixels, although at the time of writing 1,280 × 1,024 pixels is more usual with some monitors able to operate effectively at 1,600 × 1,200. This level of resolution is necessary to handle the complex graphical output from modern software packages, which can include text, graphics, pictures and video. A television screen has a low resolution of around 320 by 200 pixels and is adequate for applications such as games or teletext.

Adverts for computer equipment often describe a PC as being supplied with an 'SVGA colour monitor'. This description is not strictly correct. SVGA stands for **super video graphics array** and actually refers to a circuit board within the main processor unit. The monitor should correctly be referred to as an SVGA compatible colour monitor.

The output from the main processor unit has to be translated into a format which the monitor can understand and display. This is the function of the circuit board that is known as a video card, video display adapter or the **graphics card**.

The video or graphics cards you are most likely to meet are the **VGA** (video graphics adapter), which can provide a full colour display with a resolution of 320 × 200 pixels and the SVGA (super video graphics adapter) which gives a full colour display with a resolution of 1,024 × 768 pixels. Older machines used the MDA (monochrome display adapter) with monochrome monitors, the CGA (colour graphics adapter) and the EGA (enhanced graphics adapter) which give a lower resolution colour display.

At the time of writing there are many graphics cards that can deliver much better quality resolution than the figures given here. Some are able to give maximum resolution of 2,048 × 1,536 at 75Hz. See below for refresh rates.

Laptop computers need small, flat screens. Many use liquid crystal displays that are made of two thin sheets of glass with liquid crystals between them. These crystals alter in their ability to transmit or absorb light when a current is passed through. Using small dots of light and dark areas an image is built up and displayed on the screen.

Another element of screen displays that affects the clarity and acceptance of the image is called the **refresh rate**. This is the speed with which the screen image is redrawn to enable items to be moved and changed. Every time you input a character to a text document you will wish it to be almost immediately visible on screen.

The refresh rate of a screen is measured in **hertz**, each hertz is a cycle per second. If the refresh rate is not fast enough you will notice a flickering. For most people a refresh rate of 75Hz will be flicker free.

The refreshing is done along the lines of the display. A whole line of pixels will be redrawn. On some monitors this will be done on line one, then line three, then line five, and so on. The next scan will be on the even numbered lines. This is called an **interlaced scan** and is a cheap method to employ. It is the method used on television monitors.

Many modern PC screens are described as **non-interlaced**, these will scan each line in turn, line one followed by line two, etc.

Sound output

One of the components of the main processor unit is an audio speaker that makes audio output possible. A wide range of recorded sound effects is possible. These include simple bleeps which can be used as warnings if the user makes a mistake and more complex sound effects such as bird song and ticking clocks. These sounds are prerecorded and can be selected by the user.

Sound output is an important part of multimedia systems. These systems combine text, sound, pictures, music and video to present information to the user. An example of a multimedia system with which you may be familiar is Microsoft® Encarta®. This is an encyclopaedia system in which the text is enhanced with photographs, video and sound. If you are looking for information about, say, a musical instrument such as a flute, not only can you read about the instrument, but also look at pictures and hear the sound of the instrument.

In order to make use of multimedia systems, the standard PC system needs some additional hardware. An extra circuit board, known as a sound card is required. The sound card is plugged into one of the expansion slots of the motherboard and carries the electronic circuitry needed to process the sound information. Suitable speakers are also required to give the appropriate quality of sound output. A CD-ROM drive is also needed because multimedia systems are large and are supplied on CD-ROM disks.

Another form of sound output is speech or voice output. The output may consist of prerecorded speech. A limited number of words and phrases are stored in digital format and can be played back when required. This type of output is used by some telephone exchange systems. An example you may have used yourself is the BT Call Return system. By dialling the appropriate code, you can hear a message that tells you the telephone number of the last person to phone you. The telephone number has been stored on the exchange computer system and when you request the information it is retrieved and the message you hear is created by stringing together the appropriate prerecorded words.

Speech synthesis systems attempt to reproduce speech, rather than relying on prerecorded sounds. Using one of these systems, you might type a sentence and then the computer would 'read' it back to you. These systems store the sound fragments that are associated with different letter combinations and build up the words from these fragments. The speech produced tends to be recognisable but rather mechanical. Problems can occur with words that have similar spellings but different sounds such as bough and enough. This form of output can be used by people who do not have the ability to speak. One such example is the system used by the physicist and astronomer Stephen Hawking. He is almost paralysed by motor neurone disease. He communicates, and indeed teaches, by means of a speech synthesis system which converts the text he types into speech.

Printers

Printers are used to produce permanent output from computer systems. Printed output is also known as hard copy output.

There are two main types of printer that are used with standalone computer systems:

- Character printers
- Page printers

Character printers are printers that print output one character at a time. The character printers you are most likely to encounter are dot matrix printers and ink jet printers.

Page printers print an entire page at a time. The most common type of page printer is the laser printer.

Dot matrix printer

A dot matrix printer is shown in Figure 3.9. The paper passes over a cylindrical roller or platen that has a ribbon in front of it. The print head moves across in front of the ribbon and the characters are printed when the print head presses the ribbon against the paper. The print head contains a series of steel pins or wires arranged in one or two vertical lines. The number of pins varies from nine to as many as 48. The shapes of the characters are produced by pushing forward the appropriate pins as the head moves across the paper.

The printed characters are therefore composed of small dots of ink, so the more pins that are used, the clearer the characters will be. Most dot matrix printers can be used in either draft mode or **near letter quality** (NLQ) mode. In draft mode, the characters are printed once and are of lower quality. In NLQ mode, the characters are printed twice to give a much better quality of print. The flexibility of the print head means that a wide range of text and graphic characters can be printed using dot matrix printers.

Dot matrix printers are inexpensive and can print at speeds of up to 200 characters per second. Their main disadvantage is that they are noisy. This is because the print head is hammered very rapidly against the paper. Printers in which the print head actually makes physical contact with the paper are known as impact printers.

The dot matrix printer shown in Figure 3.9 is printing on continuous stationery. This is paper in which the sheets are joined together by perforations. Down the sides

Fig. 3.9 A dot matrix printer

of the paper are rows of sprocket holes that are used to pull the paper through the printer using a tractor feed mechanism.

Some dot matrix printers can also use single sheets of paper. In this case, a friction feed mechanism is used in which a hard rubber roller presses against the paper and pushes it through the printer. With friction feed, the paper must be fed into the printer either by hand or by means of a device known as a sheet feeder.

Today the dot matrix printer is used mainly in those situations where output to multipart NCR (no carbon required) forms such as payslips is needed.

Ink jet printers

The ink jet or bubble jet printer is basically a non-impact dot matrix printer. Tiny droplets of ink are sprayed onto the paper from the print head. The paper used must be of high quality to prevent the print 'bleeding'. Figures 3.10 and 3.11 show two examples of ink jet printers. The ThinkJet printer is a small and inexpensive version which would be used for draft quality printing. The DeskJet printer is a more expensive and sophisticated printer which can be used to produce very high quality text and graphic output. Both black and white and colour printing is possible. Very high print speeds are possible and because these printers are non-impact printers they are very quiet in operation. The DeskJet printer includes a paper hopper that allows single sheets of paper to be fed automatically into the printer. In Figure 3.11, the printer is open, to display the ink cartridges. The right-hand cartridge is used for colour printing, the other for standard black printing.

Fig. 3.10 A ThinkJet printer

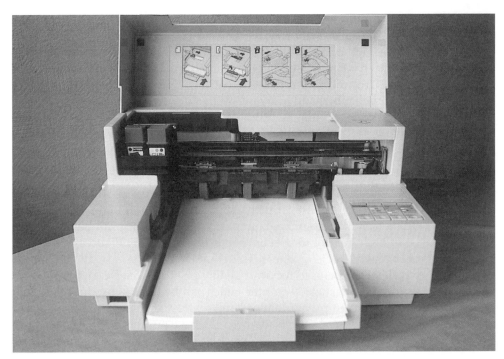

Fig. 3.11 A DeskJet printer

Laser printers

The laser printer is the most common type of page printer used with standalone computers.

In a laser printer, a fine beam of laser light is used to etch the shape of the characters or graphics required onto the surface of a light sensitive electrostatically charged drum. The drum then revolves over a cartridge containing toner, a form of dry ink. The toner is attracted to the etched areas of the drum. The toner is transferred to a sheet of paper passing over the drum, and the image is fixed to the paper by being heated. Laser printers use single sheets of paper, which are fed into the printer from a paper tray or hopper.

If you were to examine a block of solid print produced by a laser printer you would see that a square one inch by one inch (2.5cm × 2.5cm) actually consists of 300 × 300 dots. Quality of output is therefore measured in dots per inch (dpi). By this method very fine detail, high quality output is possible. The means of production also enables all graphic and character fonts to be printed. Laser printers can print in black and white or colour.

Activity

How will the laser printer produce colour output? How much are colour laser printers compared to colour inkjet printers?

As well as producing high quality output, laser printers also have other advantages. They are fast printers. Small printers, suitable for use with microcomputers, can print at speeds of between four and 16 pages per minute. Because they are non-impact printers they also have the advantage of being very quiet, which is important in busy office environments.

However, the major disadvantage of the laser printer is the cost. They are more expensive to buy than dot matrix or ink jet printers and their running costs are also higher. Toner cartridges need regular replacing – and cost more than the ribbons used with dot matrix printers and the ink cartridges needed by ink jet printers. Also, the light sensitive drum used to form the image needs to be replaced from time to time. The paper used in a laser printer must be of high quality and glazed to prevent fire in the machine. For this reason, many organisations restrict the use of laser printers. It is more economical to use ink jet printers to produce draft copies of work, with only the final copy being printed on a laser printer.

Graph plotters

These are specialist devices designed to produce charts, drawings, maps and other forms of graphical output. There are two main types:

- Flat bed
- Drum

Flat bed plotters

These plotters look like a draughting board with pens mounted on a carriage which moves along guide tracks. The paper is placed on the 'bed', held in place by suction. The pens can be raised or lowered as the image being created requires, and different coloured pens can be brought into use at various stages of the process.

Drum plotters

These have a different drawing mechanism. Instead of the paper remaining still, it moves to produce forwards and backwards movements of the pen, while the pens move from side to side or up and down, on and off the paper. Drum plotters have an advantage over flat bed plotters as they allow larger sheets of paper to be used.

All graph plotters are slow and may be used off-line. A program will be used to produce a graph/design, then the information written to disk or tape. The drawing is then produced later under the control of a small processor, sometimes called a reader.

Software

We have talked about the physical parts that make up a computer system – the hardware. Software is the name given to the instruction set that controls all this hardware. Without the software the hardware is just a pile of expensive junk. Many of you will have used software, perhaps unwittingly. It is the software that has the instruction set the machine needs to allow you to:

- Play the latest games
- Produce really professional looking letters
- 'Surf the net'

There are two different types of software: operations software and applications software.

The operations software exists to enable the various parts of the hardware to perform their useful functions. The applications software allows the user to perform more useful tasks, e.g. write a letter. All this software consists of suites (groups) of programs that work together to carry out particular tasks. A program is a set of instructions that are composed to solve a particular problem.

Operating system

First let us look at the operations software. This controls the input and output devices (collectively called **peripherals**) and the main processing unit. It is known as the **operating system** (OS).

When you first turn a computer on the **basic input output system** (BIOS) is triggered. This enables the rest of the operating system to use the particular facilities of the hardware in use.

Standalone computer systems started to be practical with the introduction of the operating system known as DOS. This stands for **disk operating system**.

The operating system has specified tasks including:

- File management
- Managing hardware resources, e.g. peripheral devices
- Providing a method of communication between the user and the machine
- Protection of hardware, software and data from damage, either accidental or malicious
- Loading of applications
- Responding to such errors as arise

File management is the manner in which the files are arranged. The view to the user is that files are organised into groups and are stored in these groups, called **directories** or **folders**. The first directory or folder is called the **root** and is usually named the same as the hard drive label; often the hard drive is labelled C. So we have a root directory called C.

Activity

Look at the 'root' on the machine available to you. You may be running Microsoft ® Windows in which case you will double click on the My Computer icon on the desktop. What is displayed on your screen?

Figure 3.12 shows a floppy drive called A and two further drives labelled C and D. There is also a removable disk drive called E and a CD drive called F. It is a conven-

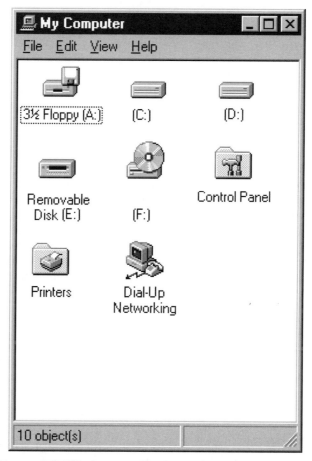

Fig. 3.12 Microsoft® Windows – My Computer contents

tion in the computing world not to call the hard drive B but to use that for another floppy drive. Some machines are equipped with two floppy drives. Historically there might have been a 5¼ inch and a 3½ inch floppy drive.

Most computers have the operations software stored on the C drive. Double click the icon for the C drive and see where that is. If you are using a computer running Microsoft ® Windows it will be contained in a folder called 'Windows'.

In this folder are kept files that contain the instructions that make up the operating system. Some folders have subfolders. This occurs when it is more practical to subdivide a large unit into smaller pieces.

Activity

Consider a traditional filing system. An insurance broker has many customers. In what way might the customer files be further subdivided?

If you are using a system with Microsoft ® Windows 3.x you will load File Manager. This will show a graphic image of the root, with all subfolders off this.

If you use Microsoft ® Windows 95 or 98 or Windows NT ® you will load Windows Explorer, which will also show the available storage devices and the various folders in each.

If you were using a machine loaded with DOS at the **command prompt** you would enter a command such as:

```
Tree|more
```

This will then show a list of all the directories and subdirectories on the root C.

The operating system will handle communications to and from the various peripherals and ensure the correct signals go to the correct part of the machine. Should you wish to send data to be printed the operating system will tell the printer to prepare to accept this. It will send your document to the printer and then let you know when the printer announces it has finished. To do this the operating system uses a piece of software called the **printer driver**. The computer must have the correct driver loaded otherwise it will not be able to send the correct signals. What is sent will be misinterpreted by the printer and the output will be gobbledegook.

Activity

Investigate your computer and see where the printer is indicated. In Microsoft ® Windows it is in the Settings section of the Start menu.

DOS systems provided a very basic interface for the user to communicate with the machinery. Usually this consisted of a plain screen with a few characters in the top left-hand corner, these are known as the prompt. The prompt on many PCs will appear as, 'C:\>'. This indicates that the machine is reading from the disk drive known as C. Most often this is the hard disk drive (see earlier) of the machine. Floppy disk drives are commonly labelled A.

DOS is known as a **command** operating system. There are various safeguards that are operated by the operating system to help prevent the loss of important data. For example, it is possible with most modern operating systems to undelete a file that has been unwittingly deleted.

The operating system provides the user with commands that enable the loading of applications software, the files for which will usually be placed into new folders specifically for the application.

The operating system will deal with many error situations for the user or notify the user of their existence, e.g. the printer may not be switched on when the user wants to use it; the user will be informed that the printer is off-line.

Unless the user was well trained they had difficulty in achieving their object. In recognition of this DOS systems are being replaced with a more user friendly environment. These are based upon the principle that the user will use the mouse to move the cursor on the screen to choose the services that they require.

These are called **graphical user interfaces** (GUI). The Microsoft ® Windows is a popular GUI. Many applications available today are run through the Windows environment, using similar screen layouts and demanding that the user manoeuvre a pointer (called the cursor) around the screen by means of a mouse (see page 110). The user then selects the activity required by 'clicking' the mouse button on an icon (picture). This working environment using **windows**, **icons**, **mouse** and **pointers** is called WIMP.

Activity

What other operating systems are available for use on PCs?

Settings

You may wish to change various settings to make it easier for you to operate the computer. Look at Figure 3.12 on page 133; there is a folder labelled Control Panel. Within this are the many areas of the computer that can be altered including:

- Date
- Time
- Monitor
- Modem
- Mouse
- Other devices as attached

When setting up a computer it is necessary to set the time and date. This enables applications software to access this in applying automated features such as a date field in a letter. Microsoft ® Windows also enables you to select different time zones from around the world.

Activity

Using the machine available to you, how do you change the date or time?

The mouse settings sometimes need adjusting to suit different users as might the monitor settings.

Activity

Investigate the settings available on the computer you use.

User ID and passwords

We have talked of the operating system running the PC. Operating systems are also used in running groups of computers that communicate with each other, called a network.

Networking software will usually enable each individual user to access their own private storage by entering a **user ID**. Each user will be issued with a unique identification name, when this is entered together with a **password**, the user may access the network. The password may be set by the network administrator, or more usually by the user themselves. A good password is five or more characters long and not obvious. If you use a network you will have a user ID and password.

Is your password the name of a family member, a friend or pet, perhaps the registration number of a family vehicle? If so, it is insecure, you should choose something that is not easily guessed.

Viruses

At your school or college there will be some software used to detect and clean virus infections. We are not talking about flu but computer viruses. These may be malicious or simply mischievous.

Viruses are small computer programs that replicate themselves and attach themselves to other programs, causing damage to the stored data. They may be passed from machine to machine via infected files. Some are sent via e-mail. At the beginning of 2000 a virus spread which came attached to an e-mail called ILOVEYOU.

Activity

What viruses are currently causing concern? Look in the specialist magazines or on the Internet.

Some organisations will not allow floppy drives to be fitted to their machines to reduce the risk of infection. In many, the antivirus software is set to check each disk as it is used.

Activity

What precautions are taken to reduce the damage caused to your network? What do you do to make sure your files are safe?

Applications software

Some aspects of applications software are already familiar to you (see Unit 2 – Handling Information). For example, the software being used to write this book is called a word processor. Other software has a variety of purposes, including:

- Games
- Cash withdrawals
- Training simulations
- Financial record keeping

Activity

There are many more applications. How many can you think of?

Although the operating systems will allow you to write and print out files they are very basic and not good enough for most users. Also they are not very 'user friendly', the user needs to be very confident and well trained to feel comfortable in working with these tools. This has led to the development of many different types of applications software, much of which is available in the shops as packages.

We shall look at:

- Word processing packages
- Desktop publishing packages
- Database packages
- Spreadsheet packages
- Graphics packages
- Programming languages
- Personal organisers

The processing of data takes four different, though often related forms. These are:

- Documents
- Numerical data
- Graphics
- Structured data

We shall look at each of these briefly now.

The production of a document may be achieved by use of the most common application software package, the word processor. The word processor has largely taken over from the typewriter as they may be used by less skilled people to produce very professional results. There are many different word processing packages available on the market today, and in the main they will all provide similar facilities.

Desktop publishing packages are an increasingly popular form of applications software which can be used to create documents containing both text and graphics, often for distribution. Examples might be the production of newsletters and advertising flyers. The distinction between these packages and word processing packages is becoming blurred as more word processors include similar facilities.

Numerical data will often be manipulated and presented using a spreadsheet package. These are widely used in industry, finance, scientific and business areas. As with word processors there are many different spreadsheet packages available on the market, however, all provide some basic facilities in common.

Spreadsheets may be used to model various occurrences. It might be that a water supply utility needs to calculate the volumes of water that could be delivered using their existing network. This model could then be used to demonstrate the results of alterations to the network.

Activity

List the situations in which you think it might be possible to use a spreadsheet to model events or circumstances.

There are many different graphics packages covering a variety of applications. Included are the graphics available to business users and governmental agencies to provide pie, bar and line charts. This is because statistical data is often easier for the majority to understand when presented in these forms. You will have seen such graphics in newspapers and on television for the presentation of share price movements, unemployment figures and many others.

There are also graphics packages available that allow the user to create drawings and designs of their own or to manipulate a supplied picture as they require. These packages will have colour and tools to allow the user to use these in much the same way as an artist would a paint palette. There will be drawing tools, a variety of fonts (usually greater than that offered on a word processor) and many other features.

Computer aided design packages are specialised graphics packages used in the design of many products from process machinery to cars and buildings. They have many drawing tools similar to other graphics packages and include the common shapes such as rectangles, ellipses and polygons. These packages may allow drawn objects to be rotated as two- or three-dimensional objects.

Database programs are widely used by even small business to store and retrieve information. This might include customers' names, addresses, telephone numbers and other details, and perhaps suppliers' details or those of staff.

The database will take the place of many filing cabinets of paper based records that may be misfiled and dirty. However, the major advantage of a database is the speed at which the required information can be retrieved for use.

Filing cabinet and stacks of paper

It is possible to write computer programs whose purpose is to destroy data or other program files. These are known as virus infections (see above).

The infection can be detected and cleaned by the use of virus checking software. It is possible to set these programs to run in the background, that is they can check and clean your system as the operating system is loaded. You don't have to remember to run it, it is set to run automatically.

Configuring applications

While many people drive cars, very few know how the engine works or how to set the timing. This is also true in the users of computers. If you are setting up a computer with the applications the user needs there are settings that they will need you to do for them.

When installing the software you should ensure that any spell or grammar checkers are using the correct language. It is said that the English and Americans are two nations divided by a common language! UK English spellings differ to those of the USA, e.g. take the word 'colour' in UK English, in America it is spelt 'color'.

There are many other areas that users may need configuring, including:

- Screen set up, toolbars, scroll bars, etc.
- Template locations
- Accessing prewritten macros
- Automating backups
- Automating saves
- File locations for reading or saving

Most of these are within the same area as mentioned for the spell and grammar checkers.

Activity

Investigate the applications to which you have access. Where are these settings? Can you alter them?

Computer programming

The computer programmer writes the software that you use. The vast majority of computer users will never write their own programs as they have no need. The applications software available is sufficient to enable them to do the work they wish to achieve.

We have said that computers only understand binary codes. Historically that is how programs were written, as a series of zeros and ones. They wrote the software in **machine code**. This is known as **low level programming**. This required a great deal of skill and knowledge on the part of the programmer. It was very difficult to do and was difficult to discover and correct errors (**debug**). These programs usually take up very little storage in memory and run very quickly.

The next form of programming language available is called **assembly**. This uses **mnemonics** for the commands instead of the complex binary codes. A command that read ADD x,y would add the contents of the memory location y to that in x. This is slightly easier to code and debug, it also runs quickly and takes little memory. The assembler will convert the mnemonic code into the machine code understood by the computer.

The **third generation** of programming languages enables less experienced programmers to write their own applications. The instructions are more easily understood by the programmer, but must be converted to a form of machine code for the computer to run the application.

Many different programming languages have been created for specialised purposes. Some of the common languages available today can be seen in Table 3.1.

Table 3.1 Programming languages

Language	Uses
Beginners **A**ll-purpose **S**ymbolic **I**nstruction **C**ode (BASIC)	As the name implies simple language for use by beginners.
COmmon **B**usiness **O**rientated **L**anguage (COBOL)	Designed to write business applications used in financial and insurance industries today.
Pascal	Named after Blaise Pascal and used in schools and colleges to teach programming.
Logo	Widely used in schools to manipulate a turtle.
C	Developed to enable the writing of portable operating systems.

Activity

There are many, many more languages. How many can you find? Why were they created?

Writing a computer program is rather like writing a recipe. All the instructions need to be clearly stated and to be in exactly the right sequence.

Activity

Write out a recipe to boil an egg. Now try it out. What assumptions did you make? Did you tell the reader when to turn off the tap? Did you remember to tell them to turn on the cooker hob?

Remember that computers are very silly, they don't think at all. So the first step to writing your own application is to decide precisely what you need to do. This is called designing the program. You identify step by step exactly what your application needs to do. In a commercial environment this early document or design will be kept. This is to allow the next programmer to follow the program more easily and so be able to maintain the code.

The next step is to make sure that such a program is not already available. It would not make sense to write a word processing program would it?

The next important point is to decide which is the most appropriate programming software to use.

In writing the code a good programmer will break up the code and include statements telling the next programmer what is happening. This is called internal documentation. It should be good enough to help even if the early paperwork has been lost (see Figure 1.6 on page 16).

Figure 1.6 shows a macro written to set up a letter by opening a new file based on a specified template. The user is then prompted to input the necessary details to start the letter. Read through the code carefully. You will see some lines start with an apostrophe and are written in fairly clear language. These are the **internal documentation** lines. As you can see they explain what the following chunk of code does. When the computer creates the **executable** code (exe) used to run the program it will ignore all these lines.

Creating a macro to automate word processor or spreadsheet operations is a very common area where we might write our own programs. Creating web sites for the Internet is another area where we might program ourselves.

Macro programs

A macro is a set of instructions that can be set up by the user of an applications package to automate routine tasks and procedures. Once a macro has been created, it can be stored and recalled for use whenever it is needed.

When you use an applications package, you will find that there are some tasks that you will carry out over and over again. For example, you might use a word processing package to produce business letters. Figures 1.2 and 1.3 on pages 8 and 9 show possible layouts for such letters.

The first time you type these letters, you need to decide on the basic layout, the page margins and the positions of the text on the page, before you type the text of the letter.

When you produce subsequent letters, you could find yourself repeating a lot of this work, e.g. setting up the page. You will also find that some of the text you type is exactly the same in every letter, for example, your address and the letter ending.

If you could automate the process of setting up the letter and typing the standard text, you could save yourself a lot of time. You could also be sure that the layout and standard text would be exactly the same each time.

When you have finished typing a letter, you will probably save it to the disk of your computer and then print it out. Again, if you could automate the saving and printing process, you could save yourself time.

Activity

Can you think of any other tasks that you carry out regularly and which could be usefully automated?

As a rule, you can use a macro to carry out any task or procedure that you can do manually. To give you some examples, macros can be used to open, save and print files, to enter text or data into files, to format documents, to set system defaults. If the applications package has an option you can use, you can create a macro to carry out the same function.

In effect, a macro is a computer program that can be created by the user of an applications package to help them with their work. The program uses a special language to record the instructions – the macro programming language.

Most users of applications packages would regard themselves as expert in the use of the package, but not as computer programmers! An important feature of the macro facilities provided by today's applications packages is that they can be used by the 'ordinary' user. Useful macros can be created by carrying out the required task and 'recording' the keystrokes and commands. The recording process automatically creates the macro file – in the programming language. The recording can then be played back as necessary, executing the commands in the macro.

The expert programmer can, of course, use the macro programming language itself to enter commands directly, creating more complex macros.

How do you use the macros you create, either by recording them or writing them in the macro programming language? There are usually several ways to call up and run a macro.

Most packages have an option that lets you call up a list of all the macros available to you. You then select and run the one you want from the list.

Macros can also be added to specific menus in a package. For example, you might write a word processing macro to change the case of selected text from upper case to lower case and vice versa. If you use this macro a lot, you might find it useful to add this as an option to the Edit menu of the word processing package.

Some packages offer 'short cut' ways of selecting and running macros. When you record a macro, you may be given the option of assigning the macro to a particular key on the keyboard. To run the macro, you press the selected key at the same time as a function key, such as the Control key.

You may also have the option of assigning your macro to a button or icon on the toolbar. Clicking on the appropriate icon can then run the macro.

Most users first encounter macros as part of a word processing package. Document and text processing is often repetitive, so there are many opportunities for automation. However, you need to remember that macros are not just a feature of word processing packages. You will also find macro facilities in spreadsheet, database and some desktop publishing packages.

It is not possible to give you detailed instructions about creating and running macros in this text, because the instructions will vary from package to package. You should have a look at the user manuals and on-line help for the package you use and see how macros can be created and used in that particular package.

Activity

Try setting up a macro for yourself. For example, record a macro that will save the document or spreadsheet you are working on and print a copy for you. Have a look at the macro file itself, so that you can see what the programming language looks like.

How do you create the macro – is there a recording facility?

How do you run the macro? Do you start it from a menu, by pressing a combination of keys or by clicking on an icon?

The examples in Figure 3.13 show the save and print macro as produced by several packages.

```
Microsoft ® Word 97 - word processing

Sub savePrint()

      ActiveDocument.Save

      ActiveDocument.PrintOut

End Sub
```

```
WordPerfect 5.2 - word processing

Application(WORD

PROCESSOR;WPWP;Default;"WPWPUK.WCD")

FileSave()

PrintFull()
```

```
Microsoft ® Excel 97 - spreadsheet

Sub savePrint()

      ActiveWorkbook.save

      ActiveWindow.SelectedSheets.PrintOut Copies:=1

End Sub
```

```
Lotus 1-2-3 - spreadsheet

{FILE-SAVE "A:\SPB.WK4";"1-2-3";;"REPLACE"}

{PRINT

"CURRENT";1:9999;1;1}
```

Fig. 3.13 Macro code examples

Hypertext Markup Language (HTML) programs

Most of you will be aware of the Internet. For any topic in which you are interested there will be a source of information on the Internet. This information may be accurate or it may not.

Anybody can publish information on the Internet. All they need is an **internet service provider** (ISP) and 'web space' on the service provider's server.

An ISP is an organisation that runs a large computer that enables their customers to gain access to other Internet sites and for customers to store their web sites to enable others to gain access to them. If you ran your web site on your machine at home it would have to be switched on at all times and anybody could gain access to your files.

Activity

Why might you or any other organisation not want this?

Many ISPs advertise five or 10MB of 'free web space'. By using these facilities you could become a publisher on the Internet.

Activity

Do a search on your name or on a topic in which you are interested. How many of the 'hits' are personal sites as opposed to business sites?

Notice how you navigate around the sites and to them. A link to another site or page is indicated by a hypertext link, the text being underlined thus, www.qca.org.uk. When you pass the cursor over the underlined text it will usually change colour. The address to which the 'hot spot' is pointed will be displayed in the bottom left-hand corner of your browser. The browser is the piece of applications software you use to view web pages and sites.

To create a web site you will use a special language created specifically for this purpose. This is called **Hypertext Markup Language (HTML)**. Look at the Figure 3.14, can you work out what would be seen when the document is published?

Looks very strange doesn't it? The rather odd looking layout is created by the formatting requirements of the word processor. Figure 3.15 shows what it looks like when published. Not a very good display.

It is very easy to create HTML code to meet your needs and those of other users. The code above includes an indication as to the software used to create it. Can you see it? Many modern word processors also enable this to be done quite easily.

Word processors and other applications such as desktop publishing (DTP) packages also contain templates to enable you to create web sites with a more interesting appearance than just black text on a white background.

```
<!doctype html public "-//w3c//dtd html 4.0
transitional//en">
<html>
<head>
<meta http-equiv="Content-Type"
content="text/html; charset=iso-8859-1">
<meta name="Author" content="tinacross">
<meta name="GENERATOR" content="Mozilla/4.6
[en-gb]C-CCK-MCD NetscapeOnline.co.uk  (WinNT; I)
[Netscape]">
<title>hoho</title>
</head>
<body>
This is an example of a small text document
created in Html
<p><font face="Arial,Helvetica">It is much
easier to create than might
seem the case</font>
</body>
</html>
```

Fig. 3.14 Example HTML code

Look at the Internet and search for sites of particular interest to you, examine these sites. Notice the colours that are used. Which work well on screen? Remember colour created by light is perceived differently by the human eye than that created by solid pigments.

This is an example of a small text document created in Html

It is much easier to create than might seem the case

Fig. 3.15 Published page

How do you navigate around the site? Notice the hypertext links (the areas of text that are underlined). These links let you 'jump' from the current location to another without scrolling or needing to open a new file.

Using the applications software available to you find out how to create a simple web page. Many applications assist in the creation of web sites by using templates and built in macros. These may be called Assistants or Wizards.

Activity

Examine all the applications software available to you. Which offer the facility to create HTML code? Can you just enter your text onto the document as if you were word processing?

Activity

Create a sample web site for your favourite sport or pop star. The software that you used to view the Internet earlier is called a browser. Use this browser to view your sample web site. Does it look as you expected? Are there changes you need to make?

Standard ways of working

Essentially all you need to understand about the standard ways of working are detailed in Unit 1 – Presenting Information. But let's do a brief recap.

To develop standard ways of working you need to work methodically. This will also help you ensure that your evidence is well presented for your portfolio.

You will usually be given a deadline for the presentation of your work for assessment. To ensure you can achieve the deadline you will need to plan your work. It is in the nature of many of us to leave things to the last minute, but we seldom do our best in a rush. Bits will be skimped or missed out completely.

There are many ways in which you can save time and one of them is to learn from your mistakes and difficulties. To help you in this try keeping a log or journal of any problems you encounter. Together with the problem you should enter the solution you found. The next time you encounter that or a similar problem you may not remember the precise solution, but you can look it up. This is a great time saving device and is very easy to do.

Each time you finish a piece of work take a critical look at it. This is called evaluating your work. What were you asked to do? How has your work fulfilled each requirement? If you were to improve the work, what would you do?

It is very important that each piece you present is carefully produced. As we have said it is very irritating to have to try to read pieces that are poorly spelt or have major grammatical errors. Carefully read your material on-screen, remember that you will tend to read what you expect to see, so beware. Use the built in spell and grammar checker, but don't just click OK. Make sure the suggestions make sense.

The suggestions made by grammar checkers in particular can completely change the meaning of your text. Avoid printing out numerous copies of your work, as this is wasteful. Check carefully on-screen first.

Do you put a lot of effort into your work? What would happen if you lost the files the day before you were due to hand it in? It is good practice and a sensible precaution to keep all files backed up. Remember that a backup copy is a second copy of a file.

You may keep your working file on the college network, or on the hard drive, or on a floppy disk. Your backup copy should be kept separately to the original. If the original file is kept on a floppy disk there is little point in having the backup on the same floppy or even on another floppy in the same disk box. Consider what would happen in the case of a fire. How can you avoid the loss should your work be caught in a fire?

Other than the major catastrophe of a fire, how might you lose your work? Many years ago, a friend of mine had been working on a major piece of work for about three hours when the power plug was literally pulled out from the computer. This was a disaster. Every scrap of work was lost. How would you prevent this happening to you? Nowadays many software packages have a setting you can control that will automatically save your work at regular intervals. Inspect the software available to you and see if there is such a setting. How often should you save your work?

When you are working you may find it sensible to keep different versions of a piece. This is done by using filenames that should:

- Tell you what the piece is
- Tell you which version it is

Remember what we said earlier about the damage that can be done to a file by viruses. However, you must protect your files from viruses. This will probably be partially done by your school or college who will be guarding their system against these dangers. However, you need to do your bit, so act sensibly and ensure that you don't inadvertently infect your files.

Remember that every piece of work you create is a publication. When you collect your data be aware that it may be subject to copyright legislation. A little common sense is usually all that you need to ensure you don't fall foul of the law. Always check with your source as to the nature of the data and whether or not you can use it.

You will use many sources for your work – this book is one of them. You must not copy text directly from a source into your own work without making it clear exactly what has been copied and from where.

Keep yourself and others safe while you work by:

- Ensuring all cabling is tucked away
- Checking cables are free from worn patches
- Checking all cables are securely connected to the plugs
- Being careful when replenishing ink and toner
- Using the correct paper (using the wrong type of paper in a laser printer can start fires!)

Think about how you work, consider the following questions:

- Is the screen correctly positioned for you?
- Is the lighting causing reflections making the screen difficult to see?
- Is the seat adjusted correctly?
- Can you reach the keyboard easily?
- Is the keyboard placed at the right angle?

Assessment evidence

This unit will be assessed by your tutor/assessor examining the work you place in your portfolio of evidence.

You might combine work for this unit with that for Unit 2 – Handling Information.

You will need to clearly describe your user requirements. You must then match the input and output devices together with the appropriate processing unit.

You will need to determine the operating system and necessary configuration requirements for your user needs. You should define the folder structures that will be suitable and create them. You should demonstrate how you set the time, date and other settings. You should ensure the keyboard and mouse drivers are installed correctly.

You should define the software that the user needs to meet their requirements and configure it appropriately with regard to file locations and others, including the best use of automated facilities.

You will demonstrate the design and implementation of suitable macro(s) and template(s) showing how they satisfy your user requirements.

You will design and create a web site showing appropriate use of text, pictures and sound. Using such controls and 'hotspots' as are necessary to link pages.

Remember that the web site and all the rest of your work should be carefully checked for errors and corrected. It is easy to avoid the worst spelling mistakes and it is not to your credit to present work with such errors in it.

While performing your work you must also demonstrate your ability to work safely and to avoid data loss.

Much of this may be presented in your portfolio as screen dumps and other output that you will annotate. The annotations will be handwritten notes identifying what the piece demonstrates by way of your knowledge and skill.

Part of the evidence might be in the form of observations or video of you performing the necessary tests. Your tests will include:

- Power up
- Using the operating system to set user settings, e.g. mouse, screen, time, date
- Setting user IDs and passwords
- Setting up anti-virus software
- Printer drivers
- Accessing the applications software required
- Testing that macros and templates work correctly
- Retrieving files and printing

All this is part of configuring the system for the user.

Figure 3.16 gives the criteria which need to be met to achieve a Pass, Merit or Distinction.

Pass	Merit	Distinction
To achieve a pass your work must show:	To achieve a merit your work must show:	To achieve a distinction your work must show:
• Clear descriptions of the user requirements and the basic specification for input devices, output devices, processing unit, operating system, applications software and configuration requirements.	• Accurate and easy to read descriptions of the hardware and software with detailed definitions of input and output devices.	• Your ability to design and configure customer toolbars and keyword actions that are well matched to user needs and lead to significant improvements to user efficiency.
• The operating system is configured appropriately, creating directory-folder structures and setting time, date, mouse, keyboard and printer drivers correctly to meet users needs (printed copy or screen dumps appropriately annotated will show your skills).	• A clear description of the HTML program and copies of the macro and template all clearly annotated to describe their purpose and how they work.	• Several attractive, easy to read, easy to use, HTML pages of information that make good use of text, sound and graphic images and enable the user to move easily between the pages using button, graphic and textual hot spots.
• Applications software is configured appropriately, setting up file locations, toolbars, backup timing, spell checker, macro and template correctly to meet user needs (printed copy or screen dumps appropriately annotated will show your skills).	• Skilled and efficient use of the operating system, application and HTML programming software and on-line help facilities (annotated copies of screen prints will help show your skills).	• Your ability to produce an imaginative and accurate template and macro that clearly enable improvements in the efficiency and effectiveness of the user and facilitate high quality output.
• A basic design plan of the HTML program with suitable text, images, sound, control buttons and hot spots to link the pages.	• Your ability to check the accuracy of your work and correct any obvious errors.	• You have edited program code to modify or correct the program (shown through annotated copies of the code before and after editing).
• Your ability to work safely when setting up equipment, checking the accuracy of your work and keeping backup copies of all files.	• Your ability to work independently to produce your work to agreed deadlines by carrying out your work plans effectively.	

Fig. 3.16 Unit 3 Hardware and Software – grade descriptors

Unit 4
PROGRAMMING

Introduction

How to write programs

Programming in Visual Basic for Applications

Code for Wicker's World Ltd invoice application

Introduction

What are computer programs? Computer programs are the sets of instructions used by a computer to perform the tasks we require of it. These often complex activities are broken down into very simple steps.

Some revision from Unit 3 – Hardware and Software. In the early days of computing programs were written by specialists. These specialists wrote the programs in a language that the computer could understand. This was **machine code**. It is very difficult to write, correct or alter, as it is simply a series of zeros and ones (**binary code**). These represent the switches upon which computers are based. A switch is either on or off, a magnetic field is either north or south.

To make programming a little easier another type of language was developed. This is called **assembly code – a mnemonic code**, that uses short alphabetic codes to represent the various actions that a computer can do. It is easier to read and so to correct or alter.

After the program is written the code is put through an assembler. This converts the mnemonic code to machine code to enable the computer to understand it.

Both machine code and assembly code need the programmer to know exactly what data is in precisely which memory location and register within the processor. They are closely tied to the architecture of a particular machine. This difficulty lead to the development of **third-generation** programming languages. These languages enabled programmers to concentrate on the user needs rather than the machine functions.

Computers cannot understand programs written in languages that are easy for us to understand. The program code must be converted into machine code. There are two types of converter, one called an **interpreter** and the other a **compiler**.

An interpreter takes one statement in the **source code** and translates it, performs this and then takes the next statement. This means that programs written in an interpreted language must have the interpreter on the machine running the program. The program may also run slower than a similar compiled program.

The compiler takes the source code and converts it into another file written in machine code, this is called an **executable** or exe file. This file may then be taken to any machine which need not contain the compiler and it will run. This makes it very portable and often the program will run faster than a similar interpreted program.

Activity

What language are you going to use to program? Is it a compiled or interpreted one?

You may use a type of **BASIC** (**B**eginners **A**ll purpose **S**ymbolic **I**nstruction **C**ode). Most of these are interpreted, although some may be compiled.

Another popular language used to teach programming is called **Pascal**, this is a compiled language. It is named after Blaise Pascal, a French mathematician who in 1642 developed the first calculating machine at the age of 18. It is claimed that his father was a tax collector!

Different languages are developed for different jobs (see Table 3.1 on page 140).

How to write programs

You may already have done some programming. You may have recorded a macro in your word processing or spreadsheet package. You will do this to enable you to repeat a particular series of steps that are either repetitive or long.

Activity

If you have not already done so, record a macro in your word processor package. Perhaps to save and print a file. When you are prompted for a name for your macro use a meaningful name to describe it, we will use the name savePrint.

If you are using a word processor package that uses Visual Basic for Applications you will have code that is similar to that in Figure 3.13 on page 143.

We have called this macro savePrint, the name clearly tells everyone exactly what the macro does. When you name programs it is important that the names you use are meaningful to all that see them.

Programming constructs

All computer programs, no matter how complex, are made up of three 'shapes', called constructs. This describes the structure of the instructions the program gives the computer.

There may be one instruction that is then always followed by another and so on. Some instructions may only be given if a particular condition is met. For example, if the fridge door is open then the light is on. Other instructions may be given repeatedly until some condition is met. For example, while the householder has not keyed in the alarm code the bell rings.

These constructs are called:

- Sequence
- Selection
- Iteration

One or all these constructs may appear in any one program.

Sequence

This involves a sequence of instructions, rather like those that may be given to you to find a particular address. For example, 'straight ahead, turn left at the post office then right at the pub.'

Selection

This structure may enable a choice of actions depending upon a condition. This may be similar to a friend saying, 'if you are in by 7p.m. phone me and we will go out, if not we will go out tomorrow evening'.

Iteration

Iteration is an uncommon word that according to the *Concise Oxford Dictionary of Current English* means 'to repeatedly happen'. When you walk you perform an iteration of step, one step then another and so on.

In computer programs an iteration is often called a loop. There are three types of loops that programmers can use.

● Fixed number of loops
● May never be performed
● Must be performed at least once

The fixed number method is often called a **For loop** as the code says:

```
For counter 1 to n
  Do this
Next counter
```

The counter is a variable that contains a value. Each time the loop is performed the value in the variable counter is incremented (increased). The loop is performed until the value in counter is equal to the value n. The loop then stops and the program continues to the next instruction below the loop.

The next two types are called **condition controlled** loops. They are performed until a particular condition is met.

The loop that may never be performed has the condition at the top of the loop, it will be performed only IF the condition is met.

```
While condition is true
 Do this
Wend
```

The loop that must be performed at least once has the condition at the end.

```
Do
 This
Until condition is true
```

Using the wrong loop structure may cause problems in your program. These problems should be found under testing

Programming in Visual Basic for Applications

This section will help you build an application that enables you to develop programming skills. It will also help you begin to appreciate the potential that 'off the shelf' applications have, that they can be customised to suit individual user needs.

In this book we shall use Microsoft ® Excel 97 and Visual Basic for Applications. You may have access to another spreadsheet application that will also perform very similar tasks but the implementation may be different.

When creating this application take your time and ensure you correctly identify your objects. Use the images supplied to help you. There is a complete listing of the code used together with the internal documentation at the back of this section on page 174.

Wicker's World Ltd

Wicker's World Ltd is a small company supplying basket ware to retailers. These are predominantly small craft shops and stalls.

We are to supply a simple application for Wicker's World Ltd that will enable the staff to create an invoice and a delivery note to be sent with the goods ordered from them. However, first we must clarify the user needs.

User specification

We must have a very clear view of what Wicker's World want this application to do for them. We are told that:

- They need to be able to create a delivery note and an invoice simultaneously from one data input session
- There is a specific range of goods that Wicker's World Ltd supplies and the prices are also defined
- They need to add VAT to the invoice
- They need to record the date on which the sale is made
- They need to record the name of the customer to whom the goods are supplied
- They need to record the total value of the sale
- They need to record the total VAT charged

The managers at Wicker's World would like the application to be easy to use as they are not confident users of IT themselves and need to understand the application to train their staff.

Developing the application

We start at the end! What must the output be for Wicker's World? We are asked to produce a delivery note and an invoice. Does Wicker's World Ltd already have such documents? If so are we required to recreate these or are we given a free hand?

Output

Let us assume they do have such documents and that they would like us to use them as the base for our output but that they need not be exact replicas. We need copies of these documents for us to use, see Figures 4.1 and 4.2.

Input

Now we need to examine the input required. Look at the sample documents provided. What needs to be input? We don't need the user to input the Wicker's World Ltd details every time, we can do that automatically. So what needs to be input are those details which change every time. These include:

- Date
- Invoice number

Wicker's World Ltd

14 Riverside Park
Riverway Industrial Estate
Long Barrow
Barsetshire
BA12 3FT

Tel 01254 486 7931   Mobile 07788 975316

Invoice Date: April 20, 2000   Invoice Number: 10122000
Invoice Address   **Delivery Address**

Mrs J Peters   Willow Wand
T/a Willow Wand   20 The Runnell
13 Brewers Lane   Little Barrow
Little Barrow   Barsetshire
Barsetshire   BA90 2KL
BA90 4YJ

Stock code	Description	Qty	Price	Cost
DB1234	WILLOW LOG BASKET (SM)	4	13.64	54.56
DB1240	WILLOW DOG BASKET (SM)	3	12.34	37.02
DB1241	WILLOW DOG BASKET (MED)	2	15.97	31.94
DB1242	WILLOW DOG BASKET (LGE)	1	17.21	17.21
DB1269	WILLOW ALI BA-BA (SM)	2	18.24	36.48
			Sub total	117.21
			VAT payable	31.01
			Total due	208.22

Fig. 4.1 Sample invoice

- Invoice address
- Delivery address
- Items sold

There are some values that will need to be calculated each time as well. These are:

- The cost of each order line (e.g. Willow Log Basket is $5 \times 3.25 = 16.25$)
- The subtotal of the entire invoice
- The VAT payable
- The total sum due

14 Riverside Park
Riverway Industrial Estate
Long Barrow
Barsetshire
BA12 3FT

Tel 01254 486 7931   Mobile 07788 975316

Delivery Note Date: April 20, 2000

Invoice Address

Mrs J Peters
T/a Willow Wand
13 Brewers Lane
Little Barrow
Barsetshire
BA90 4YJ

Delivery Address

Willow Wand
20 The Runnell
Little Barrow
Barsetshire
BA90 2KL

Stock code	Description	Qty	
DB1234	WILLOW LOG BASKET (SM)	4	
DB1240	WILLOW DOG BASKET (SM)	3	
DB1241	WILLOW DOG BASKET (MED)	2	
DB1242	WILLOW DOG BASKET (LGE)	1	
DB1269	WILLOW ALI BA-BA (SM)	2	

Received:	
Print name:	
Date/time:	

Fig. 4.2 Sample delivery note

These calculations can all be automated to reduce errors.

Process

So now we look at how to achieve these facilities. There are many ways in which it could be achieved but we will use a simple solution.

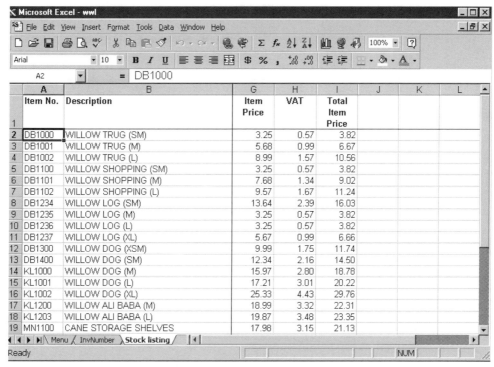

Fig. 4.3 Spreadsheet listing stock items

We can set up a spreadsheet file with stock items listed on one worksheet. See Figure 4.3.

Another worksheet can be used to store the invoice details. See Figure 4.4.

We can create an input form that the user sees and use this to accept input. From the input we can calculate the values. Having done that we place these values onto the correct worksheet, sometimes called 'writing back'.

The form can be laid out like the familiar invoice to make it easier for the users to follow.

The invoice sheet will also be used to record the issued invoice numbers. Remember that invoice numbers should be unique to the invoice.

Building the application

Firstly, we will build the user interfaces. Let us start with the invoice that is currently used and recreate that. We will use the **Visual Basic Form** for that.

We will also define some **variables**. These are pieces of memory that we will use to contain values for us while we are running the application. Variables that may be used throughout the application will be described at the beginning of the code.

In the **Visual Basic Editor**, Figure 4.5, you can select the object name and the activity, you need to select (General) and (Declarations).

The form of code used is to 'dimension' (name and create) the variable and state the name, then say what type it is to be. Variables come in a variety of types depending what needs to be done with the contents.

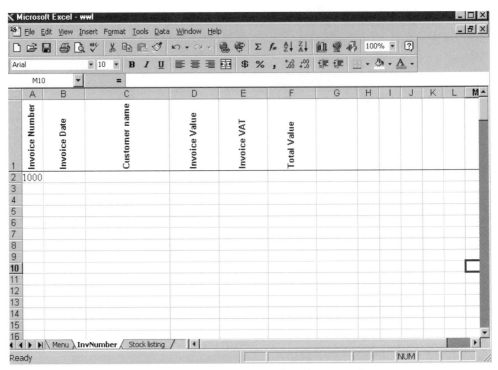

Fig. 4.4 Spreadsheet prepared to store invoice numbers

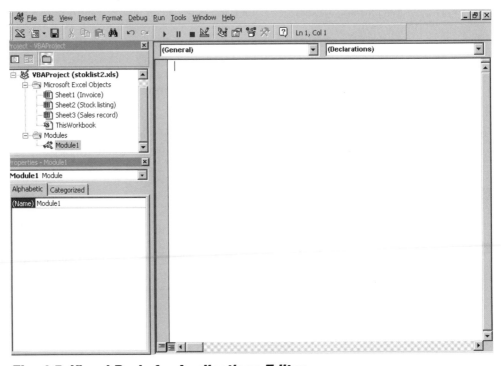

Fig. 4.5 Visual Basic for Applications Editor

We will need a number of variables. We will need to point to the rows on our spreadsheet. We need to look at the contents of various cells in our spreadsheet. It is important that variable names make sense without being too long to key in. We will start with two variables and call them:

- rowNo
- cellContent

We know rowNo will contain a number. As each row is referenced by a whole number it is called an **integer** value. We cannot be sure what we will need to put into cellContent. Cellcontent is therefore typed as a **variant**, this is very flexible.

Enter the following code:

```
Dim rowNo As Integer
Dim cellContent As Variant
```

These are known as **globally declared** variables and may be used anywhere in the program by any object.

Forms

The spreadsheet may easily be used to create an invoice but will not really look like one to the users. Therefore we will recreate the invoice and use something called a **form** in Visual Basic. We will use Visual Basic for Applications, which comes as the macro language with Microsoft ® Excel 97.

To do this, select Macro from the Tools menu and Visual Basic Editor from the submenu. This will 'launch' another application and will look similar to that shown in Figure 4.5.

Use the Help or other books to familiarise yourself with the tools available to you. This book will assume you have access to these.

Start by creating a user form. You can do this by clicking the button on the toolbar indicated in Figure 4.6.

The default form is a grey colour. We will start by turning it white (this will more closely match the original invoice). To do this you need to select BackColor from the **Properties** and click on the white cell in the Palette. Easy isn't it?

The form and all the items you draw onto it are known as **objects**. Each of these objects has a number of **properties**. Consider the object 'car', it has properties such as, colour, number of wheels and so on. Each programming object also has properties.

You will notice that the Form object has many properties. From these properties, set the following to match these:

Caption	=	Invoice
Height	=	418.5
StartUpPosition	=	2 – Centre Screen
Width	=	327

This will give you a form that has similar proportions to the original documents, a more meaningful title than UserForm1 and tells the computer where on screen to display the form when you run the program.

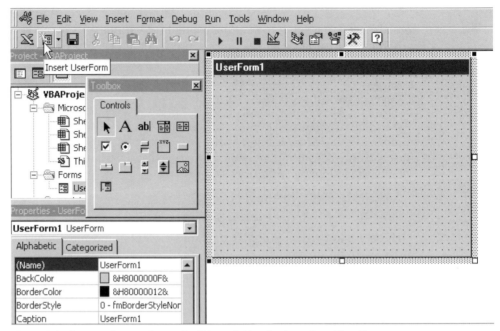

Fig. 4.6 Inserting a form in Visual Basic for Applications

Inserting pictures and text

Now we need to look again at our original invoice. The top of the page with the company name and address details is created using WordArt. You can recreate this and paste it into Paint to save as a bitmap image.

Once you have the bitmap you can incorporate it into your form by selecting the Picture property and selecting the bitmap file. Then select the PictureAlign property and set it to FmPictureAlignmentTopLeft.

Alternatively you can use the **Label** tool (see Figure 4.7) from the Toolbox to draw onto the Form and fill in the details. You will not be able to reproduce the exact fonts and layout.

Next we shall add in the invoice date. You need to add in two labels from the toolbox, see Figure 4.8. For each of these change the font to Times New Roman. In the first Label change the Caption Property to read 'Invoice Date:' and set the property AutoSize to True.

For the second label we can also set AutoSize to true but we must make sure that the WordWrap property is set to False. We are not putting any value into the Caption as we want the computer date to be inserted in there. To do this we need to start adding code.

From the View menu select Code, copy in the code shown here.

```
Private Sub UserForm_Activate()
Label2.Caption = Format(Date, "mmmm dd, yyyy")
End Sub
```

The first line identifies when the code should happen, in this case when the form is activated or started.

Fig. 4.7 Toolbox with Label control selected

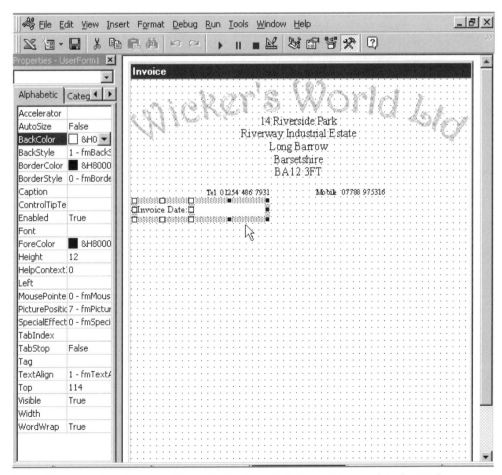

Fig. 4.8 Invoice form with Labels 1 and 2 inserted and selected

The next line identifies the object with which we wish to work, Label2. The full stop after Label2 indicates that we wish to alter one of the properties of the object, in this case the Caption. The = sign indicates that what follows is what we wish to put into the Caption. We want to put the current date in but we want to specify the format of the date. The **function**, format, will do that for us. Here we say we want the month in full, that is what the 'mmmm' means. Both the numbers of the date, indicated by 'dd'. Then all four digits of the year, shown by 'yyyy'.

Return to the form and run it. You should now find the date has appeared in the Label2 box. You will need to close the form using the top right-hand corner.

The invoice number can be managed similarly, using two labels. For label3 the Caption will be invoice number. We need to code for the contents of label4.

Before we do that, label one worksheet in your book as InvNumber. This will store the invoice numbers used to ensure each one is unique. In cell A2 put the value 1000.

The code must search the InvNumber sheet for the next invoice number. It must then add the years to that value and place them into label4.

We must first tell the computer which worksheet we need. So the next line of code we place into the UserForm_Activate section is telling the computer to select the sheet we are going to use to store the invoice numbers.

Then we set the variable rowNo to start with the value, 2.

Now we need to ask the computer to search down the 'A' column to find the last number. To do this we need to write a loop as we cannot predict how many times the loop will need to be performed (it will be one more than the last time an invoice was created, each time the application is run).

Remember there are three different types of loop. There is one that is used when we know exactly how often it will run, this is a For . . . Next loop. A counter controls this loop. Each time it is run the counter has one added to it (it is incremented), until the counter is equal to the maximum number of times required. For example, if you were printing out a times tables ($1 \times 1 = 1, 1 \times 2 = 2 \ldots 1 \times 12 = 12$) you would set the maximum to 12.

Another loop is used when we know that the code will only be run in certain circumstances and may not run at all, this is a **While...Wend loop**. The condition at the beginning of the loop will control whether or not the code within the loop will run. For example, the loop 'While temperature>20' would not be performed unless the temperature was greater than 20. It would stop being performed when the temperature fell below 20.

We need a loop that will always run at least once, the **Do . . . Loop Until**. We want the loop to run until the contents of the next cell down is blank, this is indicated by the two sets of double quotes, "".

```
Do
    cellContent = Cells(rowNo, 1).Value
    rowNo = rowNo + 1
Loop Until Cells (rowNo, 1).Value = " "
```

Note the layout of the code. All the statements that are to be performed repeatedly within the loop are indented. This makes the code easier to read.

CellContent is a variable into which we place the contents of the cell indicated by the code Cells (rowNo, 1). The syntax, grammar of the language Visual Basic for Applications, here is

```
Cells (row number, column number).
```

In this way you can identify a particular cell in a worksheet. As you can see each cell in column A, indicated in this code by the number 1, is looked at in sequence. You may then manage the various properties of that cell, in this case its contents or the **value**. Note that the variable into which the value is to be put is mentioned before the equal sign, in the same way as you place a cup before you pour from a jug.

The next line increments (increases) the value of rowNo by adding 1.

At the end of the loop cellContent contains the last number in the "A" column in the InvNumber worksheet. This is then used as the part of the Caption property in the Label4 object. Again we use the `Format` function but we just select the year portion of the date.

```
Label4.Caption = cellContent & Format(Date, "yyyy")
```

The ampersand (&) is used to concatenate (put together) the two numbers, the invoice number from the worksheet and the year number from the date.

The last action here is to increment by 1 the contents of the variable cellContent and to write that to the next empty cell in InvNumber worksheet. This sheet is now ready for the next invoice to be generated with a new number.

Your code in the UserForm_Activate section should read:

```
' select worksheet containing invoice numbers
' and initialise counter variable
  Sheets("InvNumber").Select
  rowNo = 2
' look through worksheet to find last invoice number
  Do
     cellContent = Cells(rowNo, 1).Value
     rowNo = rowNo + 1
  Loop Until Cells(rowNo, 1).Value = ""
' insert invoice number and years as invoice number
  Label4.Caption = cellContent & Format(Date, "yyyy")
' add one to invoice number and place in next empty cell in
column A
Cells(rowNo, 1).Value = cellContent + 1
```

Activity

Run the form a few times. Note the invoice number, it should change.

So far when you need to close the form you have done so using the top right-hand corner. All applications need to have a cancel button so we shall put one on our form now.

From the Toolbox select the CommandButton (see Figure 4.9). Double click in the bottom left corner of your form. This places the button on your form and opens the code window for you to enter the code. Where the cursor is simply type in the word,

```
End
```

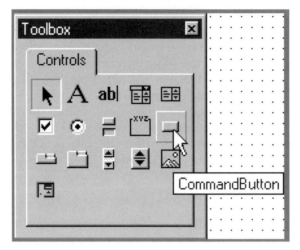

Fig. 4.9 Toolbox with CommandButton selected

There is no need for more. Now let's tidy up the button. View the user form and examine the button.

If you click on the button and set the following properties.

Caption = Cancel
Default = True
Height = 18
Width = 42

Run the form, click the Cancel button and the form will close (see Figure 4.10).

Looking down the sample invoice we next have the invoice and delivery addresses to add. These are **frames**. Within these are sets of **text boxes** that have no borders and so appear invisible. While you are placing these on your form leave the borders visible. Once you are satisfied that all is well, set the border style to none.

Next we start on the 'business' part of the invoice. There is a row of labels identifying each of the columns of data. Each label has the caption property set to show the correct values. Note that the alignment of the text within the captions varies. The labels have a text alignment property.

Next we shall create the individual rows on which we will detail the items purchased on the invoice. We will have six of these. The stock codes and the descriptions are contained on the stock listing worksheet. We need the user to be able to select from these.

ComboBoxes

The boxes we shall use for the stock codes are called **ComboBoxes**. When you first draw the ComboBox onto the form you will notice it has an arrowed button to the right.

When the six boxes are on the form this looks very clumsy. Neither do we want these buttons to be printed out on our invoice. We can prevent this happening by setting the property called, 'ShowDropDownButtonWhen' to read '1 – fmShowDrop DownButtonWhenFocus'.

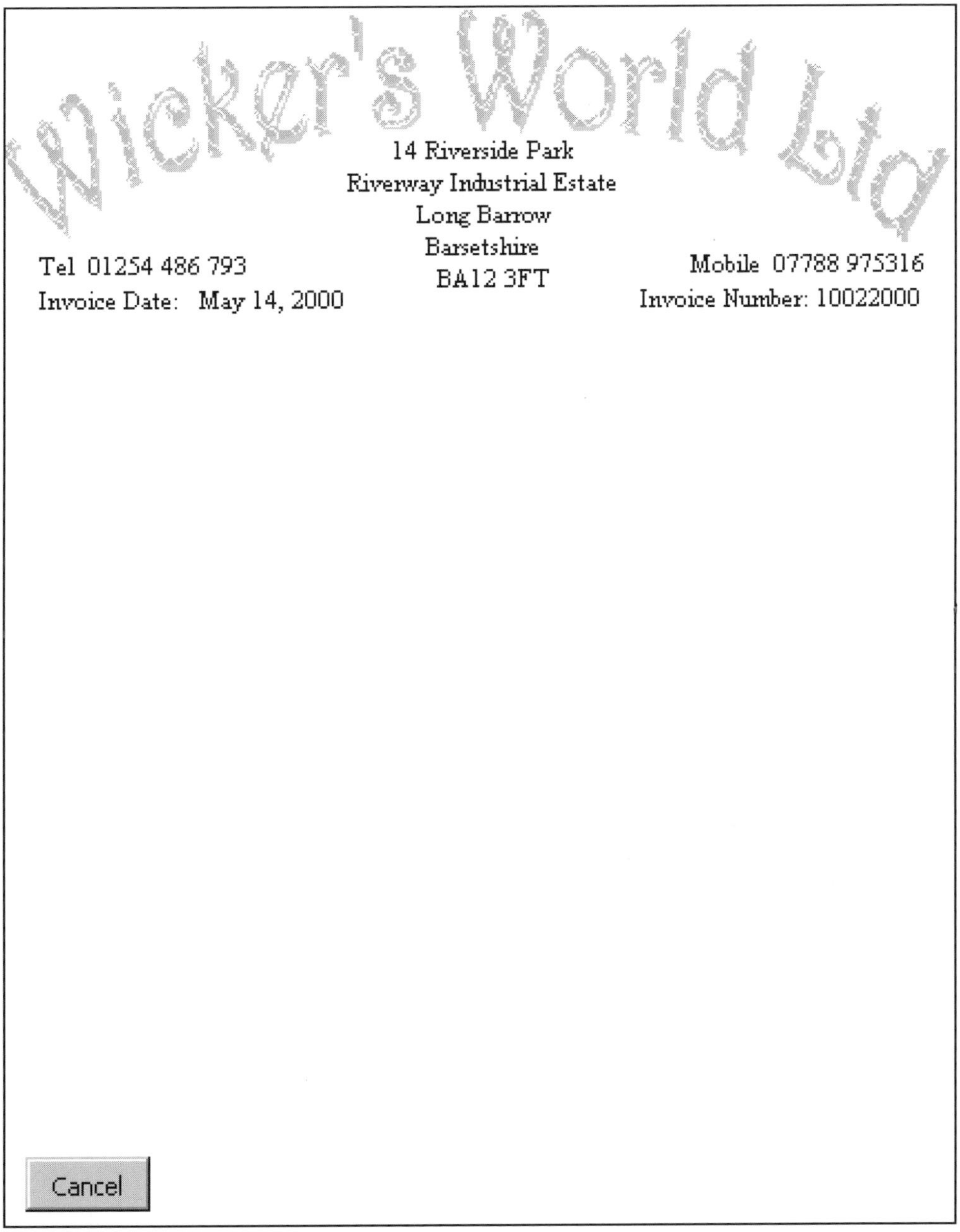

Wicker's World Ltd

14 Riverside Park
Riverway Industrial Estate
Long Barrow
Barsetshire
BA12 3FT

Tel 01254 486 793   Mobile 07788 975316
Invoice Date: May 14, 2000   Invoice Number: 10022000

Cancel

Fig. 4.10 Invoice form running with Cancel button inserted

The button then will show only when the user selects the box. Neither will the button show on printing the invoice.

To place the stock codes from the worksheet into the ComboBoxes we need more code in the UserForm_Activate section. This needs another loop. Again it will always run at least once. Again we shall use the Do . . . Loop Until.

```
Sheets("Stock listing").Select
rowNo = 2
Do
  ComboBox1.AddItem (Cells(rowNo, 1))
  ComboBox2.AddItem (Cells(rowNo, 1))
  ComboBox3.AddItem (Cells(rowNo, 1))
  ComboBox4.AddItem (Cells(rowNo, 1))
  ComboBox5.AddItem (Cells(rowNo, 1))
  ComboBox6.AddItem (Cells(rowNo, 1))
  rowNo = rowNo + 1
Loop Until Cells(rowNo, 1).Value = ""
```

Remember Cells() is a function that allows you to look at a particular cell identified by row and then column. Look at the first line of code after the 'Do' statement. The value of rowNo first time into the loop is 2. Therefore, the cell indicated is the second cell down in the first column. You may be more familiar with referencing this cell as A2. The above code then adds each item in the column A in turn to each of the six ComboBoxes until the blank cell is found, then it stops.

TextBoxes

The next column of objects in our invoice is made up of TextBoxes. These will show the description belonging to the stock code selected by the user in the ComboBoxes alongside.

The user will not be entering text into these, the text will come from the worksheet. To ensure this set the Autotab property of these TextBoxes to 'False'.

The code that will place the description into these boxes is associated with the ComboBoxes. As the user exits the ComboBoxes the form will display the relevant description.

In the code editor you select the ComboBox object from the top left selection. Then select the action we need, in this case, 'exit'. Between the 'Private Sub . . .' and 'End Sub' insert the following code

```
Private Sub ComboBox1_Exit(ByVal Cancel As
MSForms.ReturnBoolean)
  Sheets("Stock listing").Select
  rowNo = 2
  cellContent = Cells(rowNo, 1)
  Do
    cellContent = Cells(rowNo, 1)
    rowNo = rowNo + 1
  Loop Until cellContent = ComboBox1.Text
  TextBox13.Value = Cells(rowNo - 1, 2)
  TextBox15.Value = Format(Cells(rowNo - 1, 7), "#,###0.00")
End Sub
```

You will need similar code for each ComboBox.

Activity

Work out what is happening here. Refer to the earlier parts of this section to help you.

Data entry

When the user inserts the quantity value we need to ensure it is a whole number. We cannot invoice for parts of items. Therefore we shall use the format function to convert any input into a whole number as the user exits the textbox.

As before we select the object from the list then the action from the next list. Between the Private Sub and End Sub we enter the following code.

```
Private Sub TextBox14_Exit(ByVal Cancel As
MSForms.ReturnBoolean)
   TextBox14.Value = Format(TextBox14.Value, "####")
   End Sub
```

Activity

What other checks would be useful?

The code needs to be entered for each of the TextBoxes in the Quantity column.

CommandButtons

Because we don't know how many items will be entered onto each invoice we shall control the calculations by using a button. When you draw a button onto your form Visual Basic for Applications will call it CommandButton1, CommandButton2 and so on depending how many you create. Personally, I do not find these very useful names and so will rename them in the properties window. My application has a CancelButton a CalculateButton and a PrintButton.

We also have to perform some maths. This is easier to handle if we copy the TextBox contents into variables of the correct type. We only need these variables within the code for this object. They are known as 'local' variables and may not be accessed anywhere but by this button.

Enter the following code between the Private Sub and End Sub lines.

```
Dim subTotal As Currency
Dim vatPayable As Currency
Dim totalDue As Currency
```

Note the type this time is Currency, we are dealing here exclusively with money values.

For each row in the invoice we need to calculate the value of goods sold.

First we check that the user has selected goods. If the price TextBox is not empty then we can calculate the value of that row. Once we have done that we need to add the value to the value of the subtotal, this is stored in the local variable called subTotal. Underneath the variable declarations enter this code.

```
If TextBox15.Value <> "" Then
TextBox16.Value = Format((TextBox14.Value *
TextBox15.Value), "##,##0.00")
   subTotal = subTotal + TextBox16.Value
End If
```

The If statement checks to see whether the value in the TextBox is not equal to a space before it calculates the value of the row and adds that value to the subTotal. Note how we format the display in the Cost TextBox.

Activity

Can you find out why we use

subTotal = subTotal + TextBox16.Value

instead of just

subTotal + TextBox16.Value?

After we have coded each row on the invoice in this way we are ready to calculate the VAT and the total due on the invoice. These are then displayed onto the invoice in the appropriate TextBoxes. Here is the code.

```
vatPayable = subTotal * 0.175
totalDue = subTotal + vatPayable
TextBox37.Value = Format(subTotal, "##,##0.00")
TextBox38.Value = Format(vatPayable, "##,##0.00")
TextBox39.Value = Format(totalDue, "##,##0.00")
```

If you are not sure what is happening here refer to earlier in this section.
Next we need to state what is to happen when the print command is used.
Once the user selects print we know that the details on the invoice are satisfactory to the user. So those must be written to the worksheet.

```
Sheets("InvNumber").Select
rowNo = 2
cellContent = Cells(rowNo, 1)
Do
    cellContent = Cells(rowNo, 1)
    rowNo = rowNo + 1
Loop Until cellContent = ""
Cells(rowNo - 3, 2) = Label2.Caption
Cells(rowNo - 3, 3) = TextBox1.Value
Cells(rowNo - 3, 4) = TextBox37.Value
Cells(rowNo - 3, 5) = TextBox38.Value
Cells(rowNo - 3, 6) = TextBox39.Value
```

You should now be able to follow the code, but if in doubt refer back.

Wicker's World does not want the buttons printing out on their documents so we hide them before we print. Between the Private Sub and End Sub of the Print button we place the following code.

```
CancelButton.Visible = False
PrintButton.Visible = False
CalculateButton.Visible = False
```

We are ready to send the invoice to the default printer. A single line of code does this.

```
UserForm.printform
```

Your form may be called UserForm1, in which case, add in the number 1 as necessary.

Having sent the invoice we now need to adapt the invoice to give us the delivery note. Look again at the sample documents. What is necessary to complete the change?

- The label saying 'Invoice Date' needs to be changed to read 'Delivery Note Date'
- The values in the price column must be removed (the boxes may remain)
- The cost column must be removed
- The subtotal, VAT and total due must be removed
- An area for the recipient to sign, print their name and enter the date needs to be added

This code does all that.

```
Label1.Caption = "Delivery Note Date: "
Label8.Caption = ""
Label9.Visible = False
Label10.Visible = False
Label11.Visible = False
Label12.Visible = False
TextBox15.Value = ""
TextBox19.Value = ""
TextBox23.Value = ""
TextBox27.Value = ""
TextBox31.Value = ""
TextBox35.Value = ""
TextBox16.Visible = False
TextBox20.Visible = False
TextBox24.Visible = False
TextBox28.Visible = False
TextBox32.Visible = False
TextBox36.Visible = False
TextBox37.Visible = False
TextBox38.Visible = False
TextBox39.Visible = False
Label16.Visible = True
Label17.Visible = True
Label18.Visible = True
```

You will need to create labels 16, 17 and 18. Place them onto the form, overlapping the total and VAT areas is fine. You will also have to add into the UserForm_Activate code three lines to hide these boxes.

Repeat the code to print the form. Now close the application and return to Excel. You will find this in the Cancel Button code.

You might like to create a Menu on a clear sheet of your workbook, see Figure 4.11. This is done by:

- Removing the gridlines
- Using WordArt to create the Wicker's World Ltd heading
- Using the Form toolbar, placing three buttons on the worksheet

The macros you need to move between the sheets can be recorded. And the button that loads the invoice application just needs this code in it,

```
UserForm.Show
```

Remember that if your UserForm is UserForm1 to add in that 1.

Documentation

Within your code you should add in meaningful comments. These will help you remember what each section does and how it does so.

You should create a **data dictionary**. This will list every variable and identify what type of data it holds, where it is used and the constraints on its use.

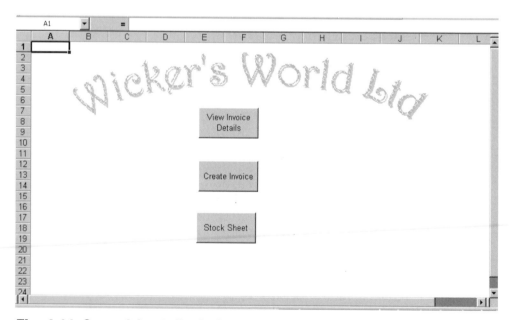

Fig. 4.11 Spreadsheet displaying menu selection

Activity

How many variables have we used here? Remember to include both global and local variables.

Also list every object you use in your application and identify what actions happen to it, e.g. the PrintButton has a 'Click' event. The code we use identifies what happens when the event is triggered. This is an action chart.

Your design documentation will include sketches of the layout as agreed with your client, details of the data they need to handle and what is to happen to it.

Testing the application

This application will now function but only if you use 'friendly' data. That is data you know will work. You should test your application thoroughly and include in your documentation what happens when it goes wrong.

Can the situation be recovered? This will provide some of the information you need to include in your **user guide**. The user guide is part of the documentation you create.

There are many potential error situations in this application as it stands here. There has been no real attempt to **validate** or to **verify** data input. This would cause serious problems in a real life situation. If you test well you will identify most of these areas.

What needs to be done to correct each situation? Do not worry if you cannot do this.

This is an introduction to what can be achieved by programming in the macro language of an 'off the shelf' package. You may be asked to create a project for one of your modules, we hope this will help you.

Code for Wicker's World Ltd invoice application

```
' declare variables to be used in application
Dim cellContent As Variant
Dim rowNo As Integer

Private Sub UserForm_activate()
' hide labels used for Delivery note
  Label16.Visible = False
  Label17.Visible = False
  Label18.Visible = False

' format and insert date into invoice/delivery note
  Label2.Caption = Format(Date, "mmmm dd, yyyy")

' select worksheet containing invoice numbers
' and initialise counter variable
  Sheets("InvNumber").Select
  rowNo = 2

' look through worksheet to find last invoice number
  Do

    cellContent = Cells(rowNo, 1).Value
    rowNo = rowNo + 1

  Loop Until Cells(rowNo, 1).Value = ""

' insert invoice number and years as invoice number
  Label4.Caption = cellContent & Format(Date, "yyyy")

' add one to invoice number and put in last cell
' on invoice worksheet
  Cells(rowNo, 1).Value = cellContent + 1

' count number of stock items listed
  Sheets("Stock listing").Select
  rowNo = 1

  Do
    rowNo = rowNo + 1
    ComboBox1.AddItem (Cells(rowNo, 1))
    ComboBox2.AddItem (Cells(rowNo, 1))
    ComboBox3.AddItem (Cells(rowNo, 1))
    ComboBox4.AddItem (Cells(rowNo, 1))
    ComboBox5.AddItem (Cells(rowNo, 1))
    ComboBox6.AddItem (Cells(rowNo, 1))
  Loop Until Cells(rowNo, 1).Value = ""

End Sub 'UserForm_activate()
```

```
Private Sub ComboBox1_Exit(ByVal Cancel As
MSForms.ReturnBoolean)

   Sheets("Stock listing").Select
   rowNo = 2
   cellContent = Cells(rowNo, 1)

   Do
      cellContent = Cells(rowNo, 1)
      rowNo = rowNo + 1
   Loop Until cellContent = ComboBox1.Text

   TextBox13.Value = Cells(rowNo - 1, 2)
   TextBox15.Value = Format(Cells(rowNo - 1, 7), "#,###0.00")

End Sub 'ComboBox1_Exit

Private Sub ComboBox2_Exit(ByVal Cancel As
MSForms.ReturnBoolean)

   Sheets("Stock listing").Select
   rowNo = 2
   cellContent = Cells(rowNo, 1)

   Do
      cellContent = Cells(rowNo, 1)
      rowNo = rowNo + 1
   Loop Until cellContent = ComboBox2.Text

   TextBox17.Value = Cells(rowNo - 1, 2)
   TextBox19.Value = Format(Cells(rowNo - 1, 7), "#,###0.00")

End Sub 'ComboBox2_Exit

Private Sub ComboBox3_Exit(ByVal Cancel As
MSForms.ReturnBoolean)

   Sheets("Stock listing").Select
   rowNo = 2
   cellContent = Cells(rowNo, 1)

   Do
      cellContent = Cells(rowNo, 1)
      rowNo = rowNo + 1
   Loop Until cellContent = ComboBox3.Text

   TextBox21.Value = Cells(rowNo - 1, 2)
   TextBox23.Value = Format(Cells(rowNo - 1, 7), "#,###0.00")

End Sub 'ComboBox3_Exit
```

```
Private Sub ComboBox4_Exit(ByVal Cancel As
MSForms.ReturnBoolean)

  Sheets("Stock listing").Select
  rowNo = 2
  cellContent = Cells(rowNo, 1)

  Do
    cellContent = Cells(rowNo, 1)
    rowNo = rowNo + 1
  Loop Until cellContent = ComboBox4.Text

  TextBox25.Value = Cells(rowNo - 1, 2)
  TextBox27.Value = Format(Cells(rowNo - 1, 7), "#,###0.00")

End Sub 'ComboBox4_Exit

Private Sub ComboBox5_Exit(ByVal Cancel As
MSForms.ReturnBoolean)

  Sheets("Stock listing").Select
  rowNo = 2
  cellContent = Cells(rowNo, 1)

  Do
    cellContent = Cells(rowNo, 1)
    rowNo = rowNo + 1
  Loop Until cellContent = ComboBox5.Text

  TextBox29.Value = Cells(rowNo - 1, 2)
  TextBox31.Value = Format(Cells(rowNo - 1, 7), "#,###0.00")

End Sub 'ComboBox5_Exit

Private Sub ComboBox6_Exit(ByVal Cancel As
MSForms.ReturnBoolean)

  Sheets("Stock listing").Select
  rowNo = 2
  cellContent = Cells(rowNo, 1)

  Do
    cellContent = Cells(rowNo, 1)
    rowNo = rowNo + 1
  Loop Until cellContent = ComboBox6.Text

  TextBox33.Value = Cells(rowNo - 1, 2)
  TextBox35.Value = Format(Cells(rowNo - 1, 7), "#,###0.00")

End Sub 'ComboBox6_Exit
```

```
Private Sub TextBox14_Exit(ByVal Cancel As
MSForms.ReturnBoolean)

    TextBox14.Value = Format(TextBox14.Value, "####")

End Sub 'TextBox14_Exit

Private Sub TextBox18_Exit(ByVal Cancel As
MSForms.ReturnBoolean)

    TextBox18.Value = Format(TextBox18.Value, "####")

End Sub 'TextBox18_Exit

Private Sub TextBox22_Exit(ByVal Cancel As
MSForms.ReturnBoolean)

    TextBox22.Value = Format(TextBox22.Value, "####")

End Sub 'TextBox22_Exit

Private Sub TextBox26_Exit(ByVal Cancel As
MSForms.ReturnBoolean)

    TextBox26.Value = Format(TextBox26.Value, "####")

End Sub 'TextBox26_Exit

Private Sub TextBox30_Exit(ByVal Cancel As
MSForms.ReturnBoolean)

    TextBox30.Value = Format(TextBox30.Value, "####")

End Sub 'TextBox30_Exit

Private Sub TextBox34_Exit(ByVal Cancel As
MSForms.ReturnBoolean)

    TextBox34.Value = Format(TextBox34.Value, "####")

End Sub 'TextBox34_Exit
 Private Sub CalculateButton_Click()

' declare local variables
Dim subTotal As Currency
Dim vatPayable As Currency
Dim totalDue As Currency

' check there are items on the invoice and calculate
If TextBox15.Value <> "" Then
```

```
   TextBox16.Value = Format((TextBox14.Value *
TextBox15.Value), "##,##0.00")
   subTotal = subTotal + TextBox16.Value
End If

If TextBox19.Value <> "" Then
   TextBox20.Value = Format((TextBox18.Value *
TextBox19.Value), "##,##0.00")
   subTotal = subTotal + TextBox20.Value
End If

If TextBox23.Value <> "" Then
   TextBox24.Value = Format((TextBox22.Value *
TextBox23.Value), "##,##0.00")
   subTotal = subTotal + TextBox24.Value
End If

If TextBox27.Value <> "" Then
   TextBox28.Value = Format((TextBox26.Value *
TextBox27.Value), "##,##0.00")
   subTotal = subTotal + TextBox28.Value
End If

If TextBox31.Value <> "" Then
   TextBox32.Value = Format((TextBox30.Value *
TextBox31.Value), "##,##0.00")
   subTotal = subTotal + TextBox32.Value
End If

If TextBox35.Value <> "" Then
   TextBox36.Value = Format((TextBox34.Value *
TextBox35.Value), "##,##0.00")
   subTotal = subTotal + TextBox36.Value
End If

' calculate VAT and total payable then
' format and place in appropriate text boxes
   vatPayable = subTotal * 0.175
   totalDue = subTotal + vatPayable
   TextBox37.Value = Format(subTotal, "##,##0.00")
   TextBox38.Value = Format(vatPayable, "##,##0.00")
   TextBox39.Value = Format(totalDue, "##,##0.00")

End Sub 'CalculateButton_Click
 Private Sub PrintButton_Click()

' hide command buttons
   CancelButton.Visible = False
```

```
    PrintButton.Visible = False
    CalculateButton.Visible = False

' print out invoice
    UserForm.printform

' write values back to record sheet
    Sheets("InvNumber").Select
    rowNo = 2
    cellContent = Cells(rowNo, 1)

    Do
      cellContent = Cells(rowNo, 1)
      rowNo = rowNo + 1
    Loop Until cellContent = ""
    Cells(rowNo - 3, 2) = Label2.Caption
    Cells(rowNo - 3, 3) = TextBox1.Value
    Cells(rowNo - 3, 4) = TextBox37.Value
    Cells(rowNo - 3, 5) = TextBox38.Value
    Cells(rowNo - 3, 6) = TextBox39.Value

' create delivery note
    Label1.Caption = "Delivery Note Date: "
    Label8.Caption = ""
    Label9.Visible = False
    Label10.Visible = False
    Label11.Visible = False
    Label12.Visible = False
    TextBox15.Value = ""
    TextBox19.Value = ""
    TextBox23.Value = ""
    TextBox27.Value = ""
    TextBox31.Value = ""
    TextBox35.Value = ""
    TextBox16.Visible = False
    TextBox20.Visible = False
    TextBox24.Visible = False
    TextBox28.Visible = False
    TextBox32.Visible = False
    TextBox36.Visible = False
    TextBox37.Visible = False
    TextBox38.Visible = False
    TextBox39.Visible = False
    Label16.Visible = True
    Label17.Visible = True
    Label18.Visible = True
```

```
' print delivery note
  UserForm.printform

' unhide command buttons
  CancelButton.Visible = True
  PrintButton.Visible = True
  CalculateButton.Visible = True

' close application and return to Excel
  End

End Sub 'PrintButton_Click

Private Sub CancelButton_Click()
' cancel application
  End

End Sub 'CancelButton_Click
```

Glossary

Applications software   Software used for a specific purpose, e.g. textual document processing (word processing), text and graphic printed presentation (desktop publishing), numerical analysis processing (spreadsheets), record and transaction processing (database), computer aided design and graphic drawing (vector graphics), graphics/artwork processing (bitmap graphics), slide/picture presentation (bitmap graphics), accounts processing, videotex systems, coding and programming, system analysis (CASE), local and wide area networking, training and learning, testing and assessment, games and leisure applications. Some software integrates several of the above applications into one package.

Asynchronous   Transmission in which each character or transmitted element is preceded by a start signal and followed by one or more stop signals. The transmission does not make use of clock signals to keep the receiver in step with the transmitter.

Attribute   In relation to database entities an attribute is a single data item representing an individual property of the object.

Audit trail   In computing this represents a record of the activities undertaken during maintenance of an electronic database.

Backup file   Copy of a file that can be used to restore data in the event of data loss or corruption.

Batch file   An operating system program file that is created to automate a processing activity.

Batch processing   A method of processing that involves the collection of similar transactions over a period of time. These are then processed in one session as a single job. There is usually no user interaction once the job has started.

Batch totals   Figure used to check that a batch of processing has been correctly undertaken. Usually some combination of the number of documents in the batch and the total value of the invoices or payments represented.

Baud	Unit of discrete signalling speed per second. Baud equals bits per second when two-state signalling is used. Multilevel signalling is used on speech circuits to obtain high bit rates.
Bitmap graphics	Electronic graphic file where each minute item (dot) in the graphic picture is represented by a single bit of information in the file. Thus, a picture with 8,000 bits of information would produce a 1,000 byte file (1 byte = 8 bits). These files cannot be scaled in the same way vector files would be.
Boolean	Capable of being one of two values, true or false. Logic type.
Bps	Bits per second. Transmission rate possible on a circuit. Equal to baud in two-state signalling circuits (bits/s or bit rate).
Bridge	A device used to connect similar LANs together, usually within the same establishment.
CD-ROM	Compact Disk Read Only Memory. A disk containing data that is created by laser and read by laser.
Central government	Organisations operating under the auspices of a state department.
Communication devices	Modem, network (LANs and WANs), telephone system (PSTN), facsimile machine, radio (including microwave), television and teletext, viewdata (video data via telephone network).
Communication methods	Broadcast (wide beam), microwave link (narrow beam), cable (metal and fibre optic), satellite (narrow and wide beam).
Communication software	For all computer based communications software is required. The main types are: system; user interface; and communication such as Terminal in Windows.
Communication types	Telephone, facsimile, viewdata, electronic mail, teletext, television, radio, telex.
Compiler	A program which translates a complete, high level language program into machine code to create a fully executable version.
Computer hardware	Main processor unit, input devices, storage devices, output devices, communication facilities and devices.

Configuration (hardware) The initial setting up and connection of hardware devices to ensure that they operate efficiently and effectively for the user.

Configuration (software) The initial setting of variables in a software package such that it runs efficiently and effectively for the user.

Control procedure A procedure designed to read input data, process that data and output signals according to preset rules, e.g. read a heat sensor, compare to limits held and adjust heater as required.

Control system A system, often computerised, that controls a process or mechanical device by sensing the need to vary the output. Examples of such sensors include heat, light humidity and pH. Such a system is said to have feedback when the output from a controlled device is sensed and the output fed back to the computer.

Control totals A single number at the end of a magnetic file which enables a check on the overall accuracy of the data within the file, e.g. a financial total.

Copyright The legal protection of software and/or data in a similar way to that of books and music.

Data Facts requiring processing to enable these facts to be presented as information.

Data format The standard in which data is presented, e.g. numbers may represent a date, a number in standard form or an integer.

Data storage The means by which data and information are stored. In manual methods this will include filing cabinets, address books, etc. Electronically storage is in the form of files on various media, magnetic, laser, etc.

Data type The characteristics of the data used. These may differ for each type of system. Typical data types are: character, number (integer, real), graphic, logic (Boolean), date.

Database A collection of data held in an organised way. Manual databases contain files of paper stores of information. Electronic databases usually contain data items (e.g. files) and their relationships (indexes and keys).

Database report The result of output from a database for a stated purpose, e.g. a list of customers and their telephone numbers.

Defaults	The settings of 'software configuration' or 'hardware configuration' to a standard set of values for the user.
Digital	A signal which has discrete states, e.g. on or off.
Direct access	The ability to fetch data from media directly using an addressing system. This form of access is possible with disk systems.
Disk drive	Hardware which operates a disk of storage media which enables direct access.
Duplex	Transmission in both directions simultaneously.
Duplex transmission	Using two channels to facilitate simultaneous transmission in both directions.
DVD	Digital versatile disk. A disk created and read using a fine beam of laser light. Capable of storing a three hour video film on media similar to CD-ROM.
Emulation	Software or hardware which acts in the same way as another system.
Encryption	Method by which data is made unintelligible to protect its confidentiality.
Environment (software)	The machine, operating system and interface provisions upon which software is designed to operate, e.g. 80386-MS-DOS-WINDOWS.
Executable (exe) file	Code created from source code after being compiled. This is the program as understood by the computer.
Execution (computing)	The action of loading a software program into memory and causing it to commence operating.
Facsimile	A device which enables the transmission of a scanned image of a document to a similar terminal.
Feedback	The process where part of the output is fed back into the input to enable action to be taken to increase or reduce the output.
Field	Part of a record structure for storing a particular data item (attribute). The area allocated on a screen or form design for a particular data item.

Field length	The numbers of characters in a field.
Field type	Classification of the type of data in a field (part of a record).
File (computing)	A collection of related records or information stored on an auxiliary (usually tape or disk) storage medium.
File management and maintenance (computing)	The action of keeping records of electronic files and their location, of copying, moving and deleting files and the creation and maintenance of a hierarchical directory structure.
File protection	Facilities offered on most LANs to enable users to set rights to a file for other users, e.g. read, write and copy.
File server	The computer which contains the network software for a LAN and often the applications software accessible by the stations using the network.
Flow chart	A diagram showing the logic, flow and control of a computer program (program flow chart) or a model of the movement and interaction of documents, data and storage in a computer system (system flow chart).
Font	A set of typefaces of one style.
Gaming (modelling)	Using software to model a situation for the purpose of a game, e.g. modelling a forest where treasure must be found.
Gateway	A device used to connect different LANs together, usually using the public data network.
Graphic user interface (GUI)	An operating system, or an addition to the operating system, which provides a graphical form of communication with the user who then points and picks instead of using the keyboard to input textual commands.
GUI	See *Graphic user interface*.
Half duplex	Transmission in both directions but not simultaneously.
Hardware	The physical parts that make up a computer.
HTML (Hypertext Markup Language)	A text based language designed to enable the creation of 'pages' of text and images to be transmitted via a low capacity communications link. These are usually 'web' pages and used on the Internet.
Hypothesis testing (modelling)	Using such software as spreadsheets to test possible situations, e.g. modelling financial break-even points for a

business, modelling chemical reactions mathematically, applying 'what if' questions to a situation.

Importing	Transferring data from one file or document to another.
Index file	File used to access a large database rapidly. Contains key field data and record addresses.
Information processing system	Hardware, software and data enabling information technology operations.
Information and Communications Technology System	Hardware, software, staff and accommodation enabling information and communications technology operations.
Information technology	Systems for the creation, acquisition, processing, storage, retrieval, selection, transformation, dissemination, and use of vocal, pictorial, textual and numerical information using a microelectronics based combination of computing and telecommunications.
Input devices	Keyboard, mouse, digitiser, joystick, bar code reader, MICR, OMR, OCR, voice (speech recognition), scanner, sensor devices, data logger.
Interpreter	A program that translates high level language into machine code one line at a time and then executes it.
Iteration	A section of a program that may be performed repeatedly, also known as a loop.
JANET	Joint academic network. A network serving the Higher Education Funding Councils and Research Councils and Institutions, with links to international networks.
Java	A powerful programming language that is conservative in the memory space it uses, suitable for delivering applications across a communications link such as used in the Internet. It is derived from C and named while the creators were enjoying their favourite coffee.
Key	One of the attributes of an entity upon which an index has been created.
Laser disk	See *CD-ROM*.
Layer (Drawing)	Different overlays of a drawing which can be visualised and may be turned on or off.

Legal requirements of IT systems	Legal requirements relate to: Data Protection Act, Software Copyright Act, Computer Misuse Act, Health and Safety at Work Act.
Local area network (LAN)	Computer network in which the computer systems are located relatively close to each other. Network connections are cables such as coaxial cable or fibre optic cable.
Local government	Organisations operating under the auspices of a locally (regional) elected council.
Logical operator (computing)	One of two values, true or false.
Loop (computing)	A group of instructions in a program that is repeatedly performed.
Macro	A program written in applications software to automate a sequence of keystrokes or events. Simplified ways of creating such programs are often provided.
Magnetic strip reader	The most extensively used form of automated data collection. Commonly used on bank cards in cash machines and for electronic funds transfer.
Mail merging	The combining of a variety of items, for example names and addresses, into a standard document, e.g. a letter. Each letter is personalised to the addressee but is common to all.
Main processor unit	CPU, motherboard, controller boards (e.g. video, disk), special processors (e.g. maths), input and output ports (serial, parallel etc.).
Mesh	A form of network topology.
Microcomputer	A system of hardware and software comprising: main processor unit, keyboard, VDU, auxiliary storage and possibly other peripheral units together with an operating system.
Mode of operation (software)	The way in which a software package enables user interaction, e.g. control key combinations, menu, object selection, function key control and the use of peripheral devices.
Model (computer)	A software representation of a real situation or system which can be used for analysis. A simplified version of a process.
Multiple table input forms	A database facility in which the user enters data via an on-screen form. The data is not stored in one table (entity) but is placed into a number of different tables.

Multiplexor	A device which enables a number of low bit rate devices to share a high bit rate transmission line.
Network	See *Local area network* and *Wide area network*.
Null modem	Cable used to enable two computers to communicate with each other by emulating a modem.
Operating system	The software program that provides the environment in which the applications programs can be executed.
Organisation	A business or private concern uniting people for a particular end.
Output devices	Visual display unit, printer, plotter, controlled devices, speech, audio.
Parallel transmission	Transmission of data a character at a time, each bit along a separate line simultaneously.
Parity	A method employed for detecting errors during transmission of data. The addition of an eighth bit to keep the number of binary ones in the envelope of transmission either even or odd.
Permanent storage	The data store of such as the computer BIOS and other boot programs, usually stored in ROM.
Pixel	Short for picture element: the smallest element that can be displayed on a video display screen.
Port	The external connection point on a computer to which peripherals devices are attached.
Prediction (modelling)	Use of computer models to forecast occurrences such as the weather.
Primary key	The attribute or attributes that are used as the primary and unique index key for an entity.
Primary storage	The ROM or RAM of a computer used to store data. See *Storage devices*.
Printer	Output device that produces character or graphic hard-copy output.
Printer driver	System software which formats data for printing.

Printer server	A computer on a network that controls printing to shared printers.
Private WAN	Network using privately owned or leased lines and which is not open to the general public.
Process control	An automated control, e.g. a factory plant where the flow is controlled by the measurement of output by specialised sensors.
Program	A set of instructions to enable a computer to carry out a particular task.
Programming language	Software used to write computer programs. There are many different languages, e.g. BASIC, COBOL, PASCAL, each of which has its own language and structure.
Proof-reading	The process of visually checking a document to ensure that it is correct
Pseudo-code	See *Structured English*.
Public WAN	Network which is available for use by the general public.
Quality Control	Using the automated sensors available to control the quality of output, e.g. the level of beer in a bottle in a beer bottling plant is measured using optical sensors.
RAM	Random Access Memory. Electronic, read and write, memory which is volatile. It loses its contents when power is removed.
Random access	The use of an address to locate the record which is not in sequential order. See *Direct access*.
Record	A group of related data items that are treated as a unit.
Record locking	The restriction of access to records to allow only one user to alter the data at one time, thus ensuring data integrity.
Relational database	A collection of data stored into a set of tables that are defined using normalisation methods. The data may be restructured and presented in many different formats.
Relationship (database)	The way in which entities in a database system are related to form a complete relational database. The relationships may be: one to one, one to many, or many to many.

Ring	A type of network topology.
ROM	Read Only Memory. Electronic, read only, memory which is not volatile. It does not lose its contents when power is removed.
Searching	Searching through data to find specific matches, e.g. to find a customer by the name of Smith.
Secondary key	The attribute or attributes that are used as a second index key for an entity.
Security	Security of IT systems relates to: data loss, data corruption, loss of confidentiality, contravention of copyright, equipment theft, software theft, data theft.
Selecting	Extracting data that conforms to the requirements of a search. See *Searching*.
Selection	A point in the program where the next item to be performed will depend upon the outcome of an 'if' statement, e.g.

```
If x>y then
    Do this
Else
    Do that
End if.
```

Sensor	A device such as a heat or light sensor which outputs electrical signals in response to detected changes.
Sequence	A series of steps performed by a program, one after another.
Sequential files	A serial file in which the records are placed in sequential order of the primary key.
Serial files	A file in which each record is placed one after another so that to read the complete file the records are read serially. All tape based files are serial because the records can only be read serially.
Serial transmission	Transmission of data a bit at a time, along one line.
Simplex	Single channel transmission in one direction only.
Simplex transmission	Transmission in one direction only.

Simulation (Computing)	A software representation of a real situation or system which can be used for analysis. To reproduce the conditions of a process.
Software	The (changeable) instruction set that controls the operation of a computer
Solar cell	A device which produces electricity from light.
Sorting	Arranging data to conform to a specified order, e.g. a list of customers sorted into alphabetical order.
Source code	The original code written by a programmer using a programming language, it is usually understandable and needs either compiling or interpreting before it can be run.
Special fields	Fields in an on-screen form designed to take specialised data, e.g. a date.
Standalone computer	A computer system that is complete in itself and is not connected to a network or other communicating device.
Star	A network topology.
Start bit	The bit at the beginning of each transmitted element of an electronic transmission.
Stop bit	The bit or bits at the end of each transmitted element of an electronic transmission.
Storage devices	RAM, ROM (CD, electronic), magnetic disk, CD, DVD, magnetic tape, magnetic card/strip.
Structured English	A shorthand form of the English language which is used to define elements of a computer program. Sometimes called pseudo-code.
Structured programming	A method of programming which uses the principles of a hierarchy of components related to the three basic constructs, a modular approach and modules which have restricted entry and exit points.
Subdirectory	See *Directory*.
Synchronous	A system of transmission where the receiver is kept in step with the transmitter by a regular series of clock pulses.
System flow chart	A diagrammatic model of the movement and interaction of documents, data and storage in a computer system.

System functions	Data capture, data input, data storage, data processing and manipulation, data transmission, data output and presentation.
Systems analysis	The investigation and analysis of user needs for an information system and proposals for a computer system. Systems analysis often includes the structured design and implementation of the system.
Table	The structure in which data attributes of a specific entity are stored.
Teletext	Textual information available from the television broadcasts, which can be displayed on television screens.
Template	A standard document layout or screen format. Once created, the template is stored as file which can be recalled when required
Temporary storage	Storage medium which allows the deletion of files or data.
Terminal emulation	A program enabling a computer to be used as a dedicated terminal in communicating with another computer.
Thermistors	A sensor whose resistance changes with temperature.
Thermostats	A device which controls or reacts to temperature change.
Transaction processing	Real time data processing system handling one transaction at a time.
Translator	A program language processor that converts the program statements into machine code. Three forms of translator are common: interpreters, compilers and assemblers.
Transmission modes	Referring to duplex, half duplex, simplex, serial or parallel data transmission.
Transmission rate	Speed at which data is transmitted, often expressed as baud rate or bits per second.
User (IT)	Information technology professional, technician or operator. Includes members of the general public when they are accessing information through information technology systems.
Utilities (software)	Software that performs a task such as file or disk management.

Validation	The checking of a data entry to confirm that it is within the acceptable range.
Variable	An area of memory assigned to contain a value used during the running of a program.
VDU	Visual Display Unit. The screen on which the output from a computer may be displayed.
Vector graphics	Electronic graphic file where the graphic elements are defined in vector form which enables them to be to be scaled each time they are used without loss of resolution. The resulting bitmap contains a different number of bits each time it is scaled.
Verification	The process of checking that data transferred matches the original source from which it was extracted.
Volatile	Readily changed dependent on circumstances. Used to refer to RAM, which will lose data stored within if the power is cut.
What if	See *Hypothesis testing*.
Wide area network (WAN)	Computer network in which the computer systems are distant from each other. WANs use connection methods such as telephone lines and satellite links.
Workstation	Network access point using either dumb terminal or microcomputer.
WWW (World Wide Web)	Phrase used in referencing addresses on the Internet.

Index